Lord, Teach us to Pray

(Lk. 11:1)

Dr John A. Wilkinson

Published by

MELROSE BOOKS

An Imprint of Melrose Press Limited
St Thomas Place, Ely
Cambridgeshire
CB7 4GG, UK
www.melrosebooks.co.uk

FIRST EDITION

Cover by Melrose Books

ISBN 978-1-911280-03-3
epub 978-1-911280-04-0
mobi 978-1-911280-05-7

Printed and bound in Great Britain by:
TJ International Ltd, Padstow, Cornwall

FSC www.fsc.org MIX Paper from responsible sources FSC® C013056

PREFACE

'The New Testament lies hidden in the Old:
And the Old is made manifest in the New.'
Saint Augustine of Hippo
354–430 A.D.

Christians gain comfort and assurance from hearing and reading the word of God, because of their belief in its authority and integrity. They are led to accept it as God's Holy Word, spoken by his Son and conveyed by the Holy Spirit to all believers through the prophets and apostles in the Old and New Testaments respectively! It is the only independent source of truth and grace to be trusted in moments of doubt and sorrow during the pilgrimage through life in this world.

Occasionally Scripture highlights words of truth through the inspiration of the Holy Spirit, which appear to be at variance with contemporary belief. There is always a personal fear of misunderstanding at such moments of revelation. Yet comfort can be found in the knowledge of the paradox of divine power, being that God often chooses the inexperienced of this world to reveal his truth, so that none can boast of the privilege (Isa. 65:1; Ro. 10:20)

Therefore with much trepidation, the author reveals a more personal approach in worship, by ascending the 'ladder of faith' in praying through each member of the Trinity. By divine grace, worshippers are elevated from their sinful worldly estate through the advocacy of the Holy Spirit and the mediation of the Son into the most holy presence of the heavenly Father. This pattern of true prayer challenges the more usual concept of a form of spiritual telephonic (or telepathic) communication between the worshipper and a distant Godhead in heaven above!

May readers follow and test this Scriptural pattern in their personal prayers and if duly rewarded express the blessing to fellow believers. In the event of failure, the author begs forgiveness.

I wish to record my gratitude to the Very Reverend Trevor Beeson for his encouragement and advice in the preparation of this monograph and to my publishers for their faith in this work.

CONTENTS

N.B. Throughout the script, the quotations from the Old Testament are printed in ***"bold italics"*** and the New Testament in **"bold print".**

Other quotations are in *'italics'* with few exceptions.

FOREWORD

"Let us draw near to God to worship, with a sincere heart in full assurance of faith."
(Heb. 10:1 and 22)

The Psalter instructs Christians that it is essential for them to know that the LORD is God and that he is good, (Middle English *god, gode)* if they are to worship him with gladness (Ps. 100)! Therefore, we must know God before attempting to draw near to him in worship. Such knowledge stimulates a deep desire in the hearts of all believers to dedicate their lives to serving him.

> "*There are many ways of worshipping God, but the most effective channel is through prayer, as this is the highest achievement of Christians and their noblest activity. Men and women are never more righteous than when they are on their knees in communion, in contact with God!*" (Dr. M. Lloyd-Jones.)

This monograph is all about worshipping God through prayer, which is fulfilled by following his divine regulations. These are found in his Holy Word, being recorded in The Old and New Testaments.

Children brought up in Christian homes are taught from their early days about how to trust and pray to Jesus.

Their single-minded belief in him and his loving heavenly Father is expressed in joy and thankfulness for all that is considered to be kind and good in their lives. In turning to God in despair, one may experience the same degree of reassurance at critical moments in adult life!

But, there is a danger of such childhood beliefs and adult aspirations evaporating along the journey through life, (Mt. 13:3–9; Mk. 4:3–20; Lk. 8:5–15) without a subsequent commitment to worshipping and serving God (Dt. 10:12–13). For even mature believers sometimes harbour episodes of doubt, which are generated by fleeting moments of despair arising from an inborn weakness of the spirit (Ps. 10:1). It is therefore essential for all Christians to learn about God through reading Holy Scripture and to grow in faith by daily worship and service.

Knowing God demands a foundation of total belief in the very being of God,

"Because anyone who comes to him must believe that he exists.
And that he rewards those who earnestly seek him."

(Heb. 11:6)

Therefore, approaching God in prayer (Ps. 50:15; Isa. 55:6) inevitably demands a personal recognition of his being and his faithfulness; it also requires an assurance of his enduring love, as it is only then that we find ourselves capable of trusting God. This leads to declaring our devotions to him and to other believers (1 Jn. 4:7–12). Such a mature faith creates a vital awareness of the awesomeness of the most holy presence of God, which is only fully appreciated by those who not only fear, but also worship him (Heb. 12:28–29).

> *"If anyone is God-fearing and does his will, to him he listens." (Hendriksen)*

God's transcendence and sovereignty are founded on him being,

"The Father of the heavenly lights, who does not change like shifting shadows."
(Jas. 1:17)

His dominion is dependent upon an eternal separation from all forms of wickedness. This even excludes all believers, because of that remnant of sin found in their hearts, which persists throughout their worldly lives! Therefore a full confession with repentance is not enough to make believers totally acceptable to God; for by his decree, none is sufficiently self-righteous to speak to him (Lev. 10:1–3)!

Prayer is never more meaningful without the personal belief that one is speaking directly to God, face-to-face, or mouth-to-mouth (Ex. 33:11; 1 Cor. 13:12). This act of communion is a gift of grace requiring a spiritual entry into his most holy presence (Isa. 6:1–9; Eze. 12:23 and 2 Cor. 12:2–4 *see* T.N.I.V. fns; 1 Th. 3:9, 13). Such a privileged access is only attainable to believers through the advocacy of the Holy Spirit, who dwells in their hearts. God's answer to our prayers is invariably revealed in his Holy Word, which is divinely provided for this very purpose. Therefore praying should always be linked to the recollection or reading of Scripture, under the guidance of the Holy Spirit! Each form of worship is inseparable from one another.

Even then, by God's decree, this spiritual approach can only be achieved through a sanctified mediator. He alone facilitates an entry (Dt. 5:4–5).To penetrate the impasse, the Old Testament reveals how Moses was provided with an initial channel of worship for the Israelites. Under the Old Covenant, only a consecrated male representative, or High Priest, was allowed to approach God's most holy presence. The man was chosen to be an elected mediator sanctified by God, but his access was restricted to only special occasions. On the Day of Atonement, the High Priest was privileged to enter the sanctuary of the earthly tabernacle and pass through the curtain separating the Holy Place from the Most Holy Place. There he was enabled to act as a mediator, conveying the confessions and petitions of his sinful people directly to their Creator!

The New Testament reveals a more wonderful approach for all believers into the most holy presence of heavenly Father under an eternal Covenant. This requires an initial acknowledgement that Jesus is the Son of God (1 Jn. 4:15), for he is the only one who is able to facilitate this personal approach to the Godhead. As Jesus is Lord, he is enabled to be our sanctified mediator (Heb. 8:6), through whom believers gain a spiritual entry into his Father's most holy presence (Jn. 4:23–24). The most approachable of God's dwelling places is to be found in the sanctuary of the eternal Tabernacle in the paradisiacal kingdom of heaven (2 Ch. 30:27; Ps. 11:4; Heb. 9:11,23–24. *see* T.N.I.V. fns.).

Therefore, true worship implies this spiritual approach through the mediation of two divine advocates, the Holy Spirit and the Son of God. They provide a channel of belief, expounded throughout God's holy word (Mt. 4:4). This mature form of worship is fulfilled through a believer's recognition of the atoning sacrifice of our Saviour. At the time of Christ's sacrificial death, the inner curtain of the heavenly sanctuary was torn in two (Mt. 27:51; Mk. 15:38; Lk. 23:45) facilitating this new approach. A privileged access into the most holy presence of the heavenly Father is achieved through the redeeming power of Jesus Christ (Heb. 6:19, 9:1–14, 10:19–22).

We may now draw near to God our heavenly Father in worship, as he draws near to us (Isa. 58:2; Heb. 10:21). He always responds to the spiritual approach of his people when in prayer they confess to their own sinfulness and unworthiness, by granting the fullness of his boundless grace. Repentance with praise and adoration of his faithfulness and love are more appealing to God, compared to requests or petitions, for he knows of our every need! His Son conveys the divine response, invariably through his holy word that is always illuminated by the Holy Spirit.

The Word of God is believed to hold miraculous powers. It is said that simply by hearing, it may change your life forever by guiding and correcting our daily pilgrimage (Ps. 119:105)! Simply listening to the reading of God's holy word converted the lives of many famous people, including John Wesley and Charles Spurgeon! Again it is said that reading Scripture never fails to change one's life forever. This is one reason for including biblical texts throughout the monograph; whatever has been added cannot diminish the power of God's word!

Conclusions

In this introductory section we have already met with three fundamental Scriptural truths:

1. The key to the understanding of God's word is to be found in the cryptic or hidden agenda of divine mysteries recorded in the Old Testament. These are expounded by the profound doctrines of Christian faith, overtly visible and unfolded in the New Testament.
2. Meaningful prayer necessitates a spiritual approach into the most holy presence of our heavenly Father, through the advocacy of the Holy Spirit.

This is the pathway of entry into his Sanctuary in the Eternal Tabernacle, his dwelling place in the paradisiacal kingdom of heaven!

3. The most profound truth reveals the invitation is given by grace alone, demanding the divine participation of a chosen and perfect mediator. This is none other than the Lord Jesus Christ.

Therefore, a basic understanding of God's commandments and laws is fundamental to fulfil one's appreciation of the 'unsearchable riches' of the Gospel of Christ (Eph. 3:8.). The former are found embraced in the Old Covenant, whereas the latter are revealed in the New Covenant.

It is the same divine and unchanging Creator described by Moses in Genesis, who gave his only Son to be Saviour of the world. The Apostle John heralded the fulfilment of the Gospel in his apocalyptic and symbolic descriptions of Christ's return recorded in the book of Revelation.

These three great doctrines will be fully explored in

the following chapters. Further studies will also prove that our two advocates with the heavenly Father play complementary roles in a believer's spiritual approach into the presence of our God and Father (1 Th. 3:9 and 13), in the heavenly sanctuary of the paradisiacal kingdom. For it is only there we can find the *Shekinah*, the glory of the most holy presence of our heavenly Father, to seek his forgiving grace before presenting our praises and petitions.

To understand the underlying theme of this monograph, it will be helpful for the reader to identify the following three patterns of divine worship in Scripture:

1. The eternal and unchanging 'ordinances of divine worship', observed in the heavenly Tabernacle, in the paradisiacal kingdom (Heb. 8:5, *see* T.N.I.V.fn.).
2. The 'former regulations of worship' of the Old Covenant practised in the earthy tabernacle. These were the patterns of the eternal ordinances in copies given to Moses (Ex. 25:40).
3. The 'latter regulations of worship' are found in the New Covenant. (Heb. 9:11) They exist today and will continue until a new heaven and new earth descend from God (Rev 21:1–2)!

It will be suggested that we fulfil the 'latter regulations of worship' through the '*Trinity founded in the Unity of the Godhead*' by spiritually ascending the ladder of faith in prayer, as dreamt of by the patriarch of old. Jacob envisaged a ladder reaching up from earth to heaven, where stood the LORD in the Presence of the God (Ge. 28:12–16 K.J.V.). Calvin believed this ladder was '*a figure of Christ*', as he alone connects earth to heaven through his mediation.

This true form of worship is beyond all human

endeavours, but is attained through the sanctifying power of the Holy Spirit. He is our advocate with God the Son, Jesus Christ, the risen Lord. The atoning power of Christ's sprinkled blood purifies all sinners saved by his grace alone, cleansing their sinful natures and transforming them into sanctified believers. This process of purification prepares believers for spiritual entry into the holy sanctuary of the heavenly Father.

Therefore, let us seek God's most holy presence in the paradisiacal Temple; that we may –

"Enter his gates with thanksgiving and his courts with praise; give thanks to him and praise his name.
For the LORD is good and his love endures for ever; his faithfulness continues through all generations."

(Ps. 100:4-5)

PART 1

OLD TESTAMENT WORSHIP

CHAPTER 1

ANCIENT WORSHIP

1. In the Beginning

Genesis relates the history of the LORD God's creation and his benevolence towards mankind whom he made in his image. The first book in the Bible derives its name from the Septuagint Greek word, '*geneseos*' (genealogy), the study of the development of plants and animals from their beginning. Calvin described Genesis as, '*the lamp of God's word*' and many modern-day theologians still consider it provides a vital understanding of Biblical text. The content of the book reveals a fundamental interpretation of God's love and forgiving grace for his chosen people (Isa. 43:1–7). This truth is acknowledged repeatedly throughout the Old and New Testaments, the former being considered by some authorities to be a faint reflection of the latter!

Genesis reveals the creation of the incredibly beautiful and awesome heavens and seas.

Then God made the land, the vegetation and fauna;

"Streams that came up from the earth watered the whole surface of the ground.

(Ge. 2:6)

> ***"Also the great creatures of the sea and every living and moving thing with which the water teems according to their kind, and every winged bird according to its kind.***
> ***And God said, let the land produce living creatures, according to their kind, livestock, creatures that move along the ground, and wild animals."***
> ***(Ge. 1:20–24)***

Then God said,

> ***"Let us make man in our image, in our likeness –"***
> ***(Ge. 1:26)***

Calvin stressed the point that Moses used the Hebrew word, *Elohim,* which is a plural number for God's name. This was to signify that the three members of the Godhead were involved in the creation of man. Calvin believed that God the Father's eternal wisdom led him to consult with the other members of the Trinity (God the Son and Holy Spirit).

Following their mutual agreement,

> ***"The LORD God formed man of the red dust of the ground, and breathed into his nostrils the breath of life, and man became a living being."***
> ***(Ge. 2:7)***

Therefore men and women were granted this highest honour, separating their beginning from all others! Adam was God's perfect creation on this earth! The text also testifies to the fact that Adam was given two natures; whereas his body was of natural origin, from the dust of the ground (as all other worldly creatures), being made in the likeness of the Creator also signifies a divine nature.

It has been said that man's living soul originally reflected the image of the Triune God, as the mind of Adam was a shadow of the LORD God's intellect, God the Son's wisdom and God the Holy Spirit's power, creating the '*trinity of his soul*'. Therefore in his creation, the first Adam was '*fashioned*' in the likeness of the second Adam, Jesus of Nazareth (Job 10:8; Ro. 5:14–19; Php. 3:21), the Son being the only true image of his heavenly Father. Jesus retained his divine nature in constant union with the Father (homoousios), co-joined with his human nature and ancestry! Adam's progeny did not inherit his intimate relationship with their Creator, due to man's fall! '*No part of him was to be free from the infection of sin*' (Calvin) but according to Paul, a spiritual restoration occurs in believers through the Gospel of Christ (Eph. 4:23–24; Col. 3:10).

The Darwinian doctrine of the evolution of species was supported by much scientific evidence, but the sequential order of evolutionary development bears a close resemblance to the symbolical or allegorical Mosaic pattern recorded in Genesis four thousand years previously! Darwin (1859) originally excluded man from his description of the evolution of species, which he believed to be the outcome of natural selection through the survival of the fittest. Yet most Christians hold to their simple, if child-like belief (Mt. 18:2–4), trusting in the biblical account of the world's beginning (Pr. 8:22–31). In this doctrine the description of God the Creator's work is shrouded in the divine mystery of his infallible wisdom and word.

2. The Garden of Eden

The Biblical Garden of Eden

Adam and Eve lived in an idyllic garden, or arboretum, freely watered by a river. Paradise (*paradaism*.Hb; *paradism* Gr.) contained many trees with fruit that were, '*pleasing to the eye and good to eat*'. For it was God's will that Adam and Eve and their progeny were to be provided with sufficient nourishment to live forever in an eternal bliss; a perfect creation!

In the middle of the Garden of Eden, there were two fruit-bearing trees possessing divine powers:

the 'tree of life' and the 'tree of the knowledge of good and evil'.
(Ge. 2:17, 3:22. K.J.V.)

The LORD God forbade the eating of the fruit from the second tree. Calvin believed that the fruit of the first tree represented the blissful eternal life originally given to an upright and obedient Adam and his family, whereas the forbidden fruit of the second tree was symbolic of the knowledge of the Word of God. It appears in retrospect, God's command was a test of obedience, rather than a denial of the blessings implied by their names! Eve was led to believe that they should neither eat the fruit, nor touch the tree in the middle of the garden. Yet later, Solomon personified his divine wisdom to being the eternal Son of God who existed before creation!

"a tree of life to them that lay hold upon her: and happy is every one that retaineth her."
(Pr. 3:18. K.J.V.)

The location of Eden remains a divine mystery, which has confused many theologians. Moses was probably in Sinai, when he declared Eden to have been planted somewhere in the east (Ge. 2:8). The only other biblical reference was of it being irrigated by a river with four headwaters, the Phison, Gihon, Tigris and Euphrates. Their geographical references are confusing, as only two are recognisable, the more important being the Euphrates. This was later described to be the largest and longest river in western Asia. It was often referred to as being the northern boundary of the Promised Land (Ex. 3:17) given by God to Abram in his first covenant with him (Ge. 15:18; Ex. 23:31; Dt. 1:7). Although Abram came from Harran near the Euphrates and a place called Hamath or Eden in Mesopotamia (Ge. 11:31; 2 Ki. 19:12), subsequent research has revealed nothing to support this to be the location of the original site of the Garden of Eden.

The Traditional Garden of Eden

Josephus believed Eden was watered by one river that ran around the whole earth. It was divided into four parts, named in clockwise direction as being the Euphrates and Tigris that flowed into the Persian Gulf (in the North), the Phison or Ganges running through India and into the ocean (in the East), and the Geon or Nile of Egypt (in the South) that flowed into the Great Sea or Mediterranean (in the West). These were the ancient boundaries of the Mosaic world!

The topography of the region of Moriah (Ge. 22:2) underwent enormous changes caused by the subterranean turmoil of the Great Rift Valley in the early millennia (Ps. 46: 2–3). A continuous geographical depression resulted from the collision of the two separate African and Eurasian plates of the Earth's crust. It produced a fault system stretching 3,700 miles between the Lebanon in the North and Mozambique in the South. The northernmost part constituted the Dead Sea Rift, a valley extending along the river Jordan from the Galilean mountains and Sea down to the Dead Sea, before proceeding south to the Gulf of Aqaba and the Red Sea. Subsequent earthquakes and volcanic eruptions occurred, as a result of the tremendous supernatural forces produced by such geographical dynamic processes. But on the southern slope of one of the highest mountains, there remained a tongue-shaped area of limestone defined by two deep ravines, later named the Hinnom Valley in the west and the Kidron Valley in the east. They were probably excavated by two great rivers running from north to south that joined together at a southerly tip to form a conjoined ravine, which continued to the Dead Sea and ended in the Red Sea.

The contained area consisted of two parallel mountainous ridges, a higher north-western (Mount Zion) and a lower north-eastern (Mount Moriah). A third ravine separated the two ridges; this was later referred to as the Tyropean valley, which was produced by a third river.

An ancient Hebraic tradition, said to date from King David, claimed that the Garden of Eden was originally located on a site near to the foot of Zion, the Mountain of the LORD. (Psalms 46–48). A Canaanite tribe were the first to build a settlement on the southerly tip of this area and called it Salem. Later the Jebusites conquered Salem and named it Jebus. They fortified the city and made its walls impregnable. When David became king of Israel, he captured Jebus by sending his warriors into the heart of the city along an unguarded underground watercourse, which was thought to be vital to its survival against sustained aggression! David called his city, Jerusalem, the City of the great king; also 'Zion, the city of our God!' At the time (1000 B.C.) it only occupied the southernmost hill called Ophel. David extended his citadel northward and eastward to embrace the two mountains Zion and Moriah. The former was higher and became recognised by David to be God's most holy mountain (Ps. 48). The building of the first North wall with a Corner Gate (later called the Garden Gate in New Testament times) strengthened the fortification of David's citadel at its most vulnerable point. Its security was celebrated in the following psalm:

"There is a river whose streams make glad the city of God."

(Ps. 46:4)

Some believe this to be a Davidic metaphorical description of the continual outpouring of God's blessings, but it might well refer to the same underground river that supplied the city with a continuous water supply! For it is reported that in the days of Solomon and Hezekiah, the City of David was full of springs, water cisterns and numerous fountains. According to Thompson, the old city was so abundantly supplied with water that there was no lack during long sieges, when the people were more likely to die from starvation rather than thirst. Now the only remnant of this abundant water supply is the watercourse outside the wall of Jerusalem; it is still referred to as the Gihon spring. King Hezekiah had a tunnel dug out to carry its water into upper and lower pools in the Tyropean Valley. They still exist today and the lower is called the pool of Siloam (2 Ch. 32:30)

Therefore, in retrospect, if this were the site of the Garden of Eden it would have been lavishly supplied with water! It is interesting to note that Joel, who was thought to have lived in the Jerusalem area between the late seventh and early fifth centuries B.C. (three to five hundred years after King David), in his prophecy on 'An Army of Locusts' refers to Zion, the LORD's holy hill:

> ***"and before them the land like the Garden of Eden."***
>
> ***(Joel. 2:1 and 3)***

There is another landscape feature in this region of Moriah, which must not escape recognition. It is a deep prehistoric cave that is mentioned repeatedly in ancient Hebraic tradition, dating as far back as the creation of Eden. Its entrance was at the foot of Mount Zion, near the river that ran in the ravine, now referred to as the Hinnom Valley! Adam was believed to have lived in the cave, but only his skull to have been buried there. Melchizedek, king of Salem, was also said to be a previous occupant. Traditionally, this ancient king was believed to be Shem, Noah's son, and his ancestry stretched even further back to Seth, Adam's third son (*see* page 52, Lk. 3:23–37). It is tempting to believe that Adam and his progeny may have continued to inhabit the cave before and even after the deluge or flood!

Even before the Roman invasion, in 63 B.C., the Jews called the area outside the gate in David's North wall, '*Golgotha*', which means in Aramaic, "the place of the Skull" (Mt. 27:33; Jn. 19:17). The name could not have originated from the shape of the rock formation, because Josephus (who was born in 37 A.D.) later recorded it to be a quarry ledge or terrace. Therefore, it was believed more likely to refer to Adam's skull, which was buried in the cave at Golgotha according to Hebraic tradition. The terraces were declared to be, "*holy to the LORD*" by Jeremiah, who was also said to have occupied the cave during the captivity (Jer. 31:40).

It had been prophesied that the LORD would shake the heavens and earth for a second time (Hag. 2:6–7), the first occasion being at Sinai (Ex. 19:18) and the second at the time of Christ's death (Mt. 27:51–53). Traditionally, it is believed that on the second occasion 'the rock of execution' above the cave was split and Adam's skull ejected from the crevice. The fissure in the rock remains visible even today! (Thompson)

Golgotha now lies within the third West wall of Jerusalem, which was first built by Agrippa in 41–43 A.D. Queen Helena and Constantine originally enclosed Golgotha (Calvary) in a rotunda in 335 A.D. It contained the cave and the 'rock of execution' with the 'Holy Sepulchre', which was hewn out of the rock and conveyed to the site. After its destruction by the Persians in 614 A.D., the Crusaders rebuilt the rotunda in 1149 A.D. In the present day 'Church of the Holy Sepulchre', near to the entrance, there is a Chapel of Adam and also a flight of stone steps leading down to Melchizedek's cave below 'the rock of execution'. Origen lived from 185 to 254 A.D. and was a great leader of the early Christian church. He recorded the traditional story of Adam's burial under the future site of Christ's crucifixion, '*so that the redemptive blood of Christ would have flowed over his grave.*' There is a flaw in this traditional story, in that the blood of Christ that fell from the cross onto the ground was soiled, which meant the loss of its redemptive power according to the Mosaic Law!

Therefore the location of the Garden of Eden is largely dependent upon oral Hebraic tradition and the few biblical references, which highlighted the Mosaic siting of the biblical garden in Babylonia. This is to be compared with the more recent suggestion of Golgotha to be near Mount Zion! So the divine mystery still exists, as evidence of the continuance of God's unfolding love towards those who trust and obey his Word!

The Celestial Garden of Eden

The Biblical narrative begins in the Garden of Eden (Ge. 2:8–14) created by the LORD God, and ends in the prophecy of the Holy City, Jerusalem (Rev. 21:9–14) containing the celestial Garden of Eden (Rev. 22:1–2). The former has been considered by many to be a shadow or poor reflection of the latter. In the paradisiacal vision of the Apostle John, there was a river flowing from the throne of God. On each side of the river stood the 'tree of life,' bearing twelve crops of fruit every month, therefore yielding perpetual firstfruit! As the two named trees in the Garden of Eden on earth were sacred to the LORD and symbolic of divine blessings, they could well have been reflections of their celestial counterparts that produce perpetual firstfruit! This theory might be the hidden explanation to the divine mystery of the sacredness of the two trees in the biblical Garden of Eden!

3. Firstfruit

In the Old Testament, the Mosaic Law (Lev. 19:23–24) declared the firstfruit of a tree to be one of the products of the soil that should be treated as sacred to the LORD. Therefore their fruit was to be rendered to God as a symbolic sacrifice. This command could well have emanated from an original creative source, such as the LORD God's command in the Garden of Eden. For if the two sacred trees had produced perpetually firstfruit, which had to be left to rot and fertilise the soil of the garden, then the occupants would have benefited indirectly from God's bountiful grace! Therefore Adam and Eve might have lived forever enjoying an intimate worship with the LORD God, as he walked in the garden in the cool of the day (Ge. 3:8)! Even now, it is a Jewish custom to refrain from picking the firstfruit for nourishment. It must be allowed to drop and fertilise the soil surrounding the tree!

Later, in the Mosaic Laws that followed the Ten Commandments, the Israelites were instructed to dedicate not only the firstfruit of everything grown, (Ex. 23:16 and 19; Lev. 23:9 and 14), but also the firstborn offspring of the womb. This included all firstborn sons and the firstborn males of livestock (Ex. 13: 1–2), each having to be dedicated to the LORD.

In the Old Testament, the firstfruits were dedicated to God in recognition of his grace. They were given for the undeserved kindness he had so freely given in the past, rather than for the hope for all future blessings. The book of Deuteronomy is a repetition of God's Covenant Law (Lev. 2:11–16, 23:9–14). Moses, whose authorship was confirmed by Jesus (Mt. 19:8), quoted the Law in his farewell address to the Israelites before they entered the Promised Land of Canaan. It contains a summary of *Yahweh's* Laws and Covenants, as well as a recording of the LORD's forgiving grace in granting their freedom from bondage. Finally, he summoned them to remember his previous command, in which he declared to their ancestors to render:

"Some of the firstfruits of all that you produce from the soil of the land that the LORD your God is giving you –"

(Dt. 26:1-4)

They were to be offered to the priests for the vulnerable or poor in their community. This was God's will, which still demands the attention of his people; so they also can pray,

"I have obeyed the LORD my God. I have done everything you have commanded me."

(Dt. 26:14)

On entering the Promised Land, they were commanded to present this sacred portion of their future harvest to *Yahweh.* It was to be the choice portion and not what was left over after everyone had been satisfied! He had heard their cries in bondage and in a series of miraculous events set them free to enjoy the LORD'S grace upon grace in a land flowing with milk and honey.

In the New Testament, John the Baptist warned the Pharisees and Sadducees that every tree that does not produce good fruit will be cut down (Mt. 3:10). When Jesus was asked, which the greatest commandment is, he answered the first is to love the Lord your God; and the second is to love and give to the poor (Mk. 12:29–31).

Therefore the Gospel of Jesus Christ repeats the Covenant LORD's command, to put God first in our lives and give to those more vulnerable. Jesus said to those who love him, you have been chosen and appointed to bear fruit that will last, perpetual firstfruit (Jn. 15:16–17). Paul attributed the Holy Spirit to be the firstfruit for all believers (Ro. 8:23) and a guaranteed deposit of eternal life (2 Cor. 1:22). He also described Christ, as being the firstfruit of the resurrected dead (1 Cor. 15:20–23). And to the church in Colossus, he prayed that they might please God in every way, by bearing fruit in every good work, (Col. 1:10) whereas James advised the early Christians, to be a kind of firstfruit of all God created (Jas. 1:18).

4. Ancient Sacrifice

It is recorded in Scripture that Adam was driven out of the garden in Eden because of his disobedience. There was no alternative to banishing him, in order to preserve God's most holy presence. It was also this original sin that prevented Adam from re-entering the garden, which was protected by the same angels or cherubim that were to guard God's most holy presence over the Ark of the Covenant (Calvin). Adam's exile robbed him and his descendants of many of the blessings he had previously enjoyed, which included the privilege of a personal approach to the very presence of God to worship him.

Yet this divine wrath against sin was mitigated by God's generous acceptance of spiritual sacrifices from disobedient men, when rendered as an expression of their personal hope of salvation. As evidence of his continuing faithfulness, God mercifully softened Adam's exile by providing him with another home and livelihood.

> '*Adam was excommunicated from the garden and the tree of life, but a new remedy was offered him in sacrifices.*' (Calvin)

According to Hebraic tradition, it is said that Adam was the first man to render an offering in recognition of God's forgiving grace, by sacrificing a unicorn (the noblest of all creatures) as a burnt offering. It is clear from biblical text that he also instructed his sons, Cain and Abel, in this ritual of faithful worship. Yet God was not persuaded by the nature of their sacrifices, but favoured Abel and accepted his offering to be an expression of devotional faith and heartfelt thanksgiving. It was said later, God looks into the heart of men and women and rejects the offerings of the wicked (1 Sam. 16:7)!

Therefore it appears that ancient sacrifice was originally an act aimed at the removal of guilt and for reconciliation. It was an act of worship in recognition of the wrath of God against personal evil, expressing the hope or promise of divine expiation, or the blotting out of sin! It was a solemn rite that revealed the devotion and gratitude of the worshipper, as a means of gaining a fragile and distant fellowship with a holy God. He provided the life in the blood of a creature to make atonement on an altar (Lev. 17:11).

> *'The custom of sacrifice was not rashly devised by men, but was divinely ordained by God, reconciling himself to his disobedient people.'* (Calvin)

The practice was originally based on the ancient belief of gaining lasting benefit by the surrender of a valuable and personal possession. This was either the firstfruit of the harvest, or an unblemished first born of the flock; in the latter case it involved the life of the sacrificial victim on an altar by the shedding of blood.

It demanded from the worshipper an offering, as a substitute for himself, to be a sacrifice expressing his personal guilt and faith in forgiveness. God has never been delighted with worldly external worship, but has always been prepared to accept spiritually offered sacrifices, as a sign of repentance and faith.

History

There are many instances of ancient, solemn and religious sacrificial rites recorded in Genesis. After being rescued from the flood, Noah built an altar to God Almighty. By taking some of the clean animals and birds rescued from the deluge, he sacrificed them as burnt offerings upon it – and God swore an everlasting oath.

"While the earth remaineth,
seed-time and harvest,
cold and heat, and summer and winter,
and day and night shall not cease."
(Ge. 8:22)

Another iconic occasion occurred when God tested Abraham by instructing him to,

"Take your son, your only son, Isaac, whom you love, and go to the region of Moriah. Sacrifice him there as a burnt offering on one of the mountains I will tell you about."
(Ge. 22:2)

Abraham instantly obeyed the command, as he believed God would resurrect Isaac. His faith was founded on a previous divine promise that he would become the father of many nations through the progeny of his only legitimate son (Ge. 17:3–16).

But before the sacrifice was made, the angel of the LORD stayed Abraham's hand, as God knew from his obedience that he feared his word. His servant had not withheld his only beloved son! And Abraham prophesied,

"The LORD Will Provide."
(Ge. 22:14)

Then the angel called a second time, to declare the LORD's oath,

"Through your offspring all nations on earth will be blessed."
(This included Jesus of Nazareth,
the Messiah *see* Mt. 1:11)

Subsequently it became Hebraic belief that,

"On the mountain of the LORD it will be provided."
(Ge. 22:1–19)

Although traditionally it is believed that this test of faith occurred on Mount Moriah, there is much Scriptural evidence pointing to Mount Zion being the mountain of the LORD (Ps. 24:3; Isa. 2:3, 30:29; Zec. 8:3). This is also the traditional site of Golgotha, where God was to fulfill his faithfulness and Abraham's prophecy by providing the salvation of the world! Abraham's Chapel is located on the north side of the 'Church of the Holy Sepulchre', and the Armenian Church claims it to be built on the site of Abraham's altar for Isaac! A compassionate God spared Abraham the awesome experience of sacrificing his youthful son, Isaac, by providing a substitute ram for the offering.

At Golgotha, at the summit of the rock of execution in the 'Church of the Holy Sepulchre' on Mount Zion, there is a large mural painting depicting the testing of Abraham being a 'type event' that pointed towards Christ's preordained sacrifice. Therefore Abraham's son Isaac was the Old Testament-type image or counterpart of the New Testament antitype, Jesus Christ, the Son of God! Two thousand years later, the heavenly Father had no alternative provision for the withholding of his Son, his only Son; but God foreknew that it was within his power to raise him from the dead within three days!

Ancient sacrifice was practised until the time of the exodus from Egypt, when it was succeeded by a new code of worship presented by the LORD to Moses on Mount Sinai. This regulation of worship was originally confined to the tabernacle, but later transferred to the temple in Jerusalem.

5. Oaths and Covenants

Traditionally, an oath is defined as a declaration of truth, or a promise to fulfil a pledge; whereas a covenant is a sealed contract, or a binding agreement. Swearing on Holy Script and declaring God to be a witness usually uphold the former. The latter is an obligation between two or more parties to do, or refrain from doing, a particular act. Biblically an oath is made in the presence of God and is therefore absolutely binding (Ge.21:23; Heb.6:16) and to retract is an offence against God.

A covenant was confirmed by uplifting a hand, or by placing a hand under the thigh of the person to whom the contract was being made (Ge. 24:2). In the Old Testament, there are many solemn oaths and covenants involving the special relationship between the LORD God and his chosen people, Israel. Some were conditional, demanding faithfulness and obedience.

History

Noahic Covenant

This was the first recorded, unconditional and everlasting covenant made by God with Noah and all creation (Ge. 9:8–17); the sign, or the seal, was a rainbow set in the clouds (*see* page 25).

Abrahamic Covenants

When the LORD first called Abram to bless him, God promised his servant that he would become a great nation (Ge. 13:14–17). Later, the promise was reinforced with an unconditional covenant that Abram's own offspring (natural and spiritual) would be prolific, as his faith had been credited to him as righteousness (Ge. 15:1–20). Abram was instructed to solemnise the obligation by an ancient custom of *'cutting'*. This involved the cleaving of the sacrificial heifer, goat and ram, each into two halves and separating the parts to lie opposite each other. At the same time, according to Hebraic tradition, he swore a self-maledictory oath,

'May it be done to me, if I do not keep my
oath and pledge.'

At sunset, a smoking fire pot and blazing torch, symbolising the holy presence of God, passed between the separated pieces!

Still later, the LORD made a conditional, suzerain covenant with Abram, in which he repeated the divine pledge to make him and his descendants a great nation, and called him by a new name – Abraham. The pledge was however dependent upon him and his offspring remaining faithful and subservient to their Sovereign LORD, this total consecration being symbolised by circumcision (Ge. 17:1–16).The covenant was confirmed after Abraham had been tested, (Ge. 22: 15–18) but on this occasion God swore by himself,

"There being no one greater than him!"
(Heb. 6:13)

Sinaitic (Mosaic) Covenant

This epic covenant was made in 1440 B.C. following the four hundred years of captivity. It was in the form of a suzerain or sovereign covenant applied to the Israelite nation, as God's chosen people. It confirmed the previous Abramic covenants, (Ge. 18:18, 22:15–18) and contained a conditional divine pledge made to Israel after their freedom from slavery. It was given to Moses, their new leader, when the LORD called to him from Mount Sinai (Ex. 19:3).

It was an everlasting covenant containing a divine promise to the Israelites to protect them; but the promise was dependent upon them remaining faithful to the LORD and obedient to his Ten Commandments and Law, as recorded in the Book of the Covenant (Ex. 20:22–23;

Dt. 30:15–18). Yet neither Moses, nor the Israelites were able to uphold the fulfillment of the Law. Their greatest leader had stood in the divine presence and spoken repeatedly to God. He also wrote the Covenant book under divine guidance for the people.

But, on one occasion he failed to obey the LORD's command, to honour God as holy before his people (Nu. 27:14; Dt. 32:51). For this reason, Moses was forbidden to enter the Promised Land. At the same time, the LORD predicted that the Israelites would soon forsake their God and break the divine covenant made with them (Dt. 31:14–18).

The New Covenant

Eight hundred years later (800 B.C.) Jeremiah prophesied the time was coming when the LORD would make a new covenant with the house of Israel and the house of Judah. It would not be like the covenant made with their forefathers that was inscribed by the finger of God on two stone tablets, (Dt. 9:10) but another covenant concerning the house of Israel after that time, declaring,

> ***"I will put my law into their minds and will write it on their hearts.***
> ***I will be their God, and they will be my people."***
> ***(Jer. 31:33)***

Conclusions

Retrospectively, there was an ongoing narrative of divine promises or pledges, covenants and oaths stretching back in biblical history to the dawn of creation. Such was the evidence of God's patronage towards all people and nations who appeared righteous in his sight.

Therefore, God's plan of redemption has been carefully unfolded throughout history; but it concerns only a remnant of the people whom he selects, as being predestined to become his chosen race. It began with the ancient rites of *'cutting'*, before passing through the early unconditional promises of sacrifice. These were followed by the more demanding conditional pledges of the suzerain covenants and oaths that were offered to the Israelite race.

The Old Testament narrative ends with the divine promise given to Jeremiah of a new covenant, the author of which would fulfil all the demands of a greater sacrifice on our behalf (Heb. 8:8–12). The advent of Jesus in Bethlehem of Judea heralded the fulfilment of God's promise, Jesus Christ being the intermediary between his heavenly Father and his chosen people:

> **"By calling this covenant 'new', he has made the first one obsolete; and what is obsolete and ageing will soon disappear."**
>
> **(Heb. 8:13)**

CHAPTER 2

THE MOSAIC-LEVITICAL PATTERN OF WORSHIP

1. Introduction

Before the reader decides to skip over this apparently awesome chapter and pass on to greener pastures, may it be said that anything less than a full understanding of the contents of this section lowers our personal appreciation of 'the breadth, and length, and depth, and height' of Jesus Christ's unfailing love for the world (Jn. 3:16; Ro. 8:28–39; Eph. 3:17–19 K.J.V.). It is of necessity a reference chapter and must inevitably be factual. It might be worthwhile reading the conclusions at the end of the chapter, (pp. 48–50) before embarking on a study of the contents!

Ever since God created men and women in his own image, he has longed to live among them, regardless of their inherent and acquired sinfulness. God promised Moses that his divine presence would go with him *(Ex. 33:14)*. This commitment was made initially for the duration of the Israelites' journey in the desert to the Promised Land! The LORD revealed to Moses the plan to fulfill his holy desire for communion with his chosen people. It was intended for man to respond to God's awesome presence, by following a copy of the 'ordinances of divine worship' (Ex. 25:40; Heb. 8:5, *see* T.N.I.V. fn. 9:23, 10:1) that were destined to continue throughout eternity! Every detail was to be repeated, to encourage the people to seek an approach to God's most holy presence. Bringing their offerings to his sanctuary allowed them to,

> ***"Worship the LORD with gladness - give thanks to him and praise his name."***
> ***(Ps. 100:2–4)***

To fulfill the divine plan, God realized that it was necessary to ordain a group of people, creating a priestly order to lead the Hebrew nation in worship. Moses was instructed to make Aaron and his sons priests and to appoint their Levite tribe as assistants in the work of the tabernacle (Ex.28:1; Lev.21:1–22). In his infinite wisdom God chose this truculent tribe, their father being Jacob's third son Levi, who with his brother Simeon were considered to be angry and cruel. The Levites were judged unfit to be allotted land under Jacob's settlement of Canaan (Ge.49:7), which led to the tribe being scattered and dispersed throughout Israel. Yet they were chosen to become the ordained establishment of the Hebrew race (Nu.3:5–10,49) and to be blessed with the priestly privileges of serving God's devotions in the sanctuary of the tabernacle under the ritual of the Levitical system.

The Mosaic priesthood was responsible for the Hebrew worship under God's law of holiness (Ro.7:12), God's Word for generations to come. Therefore the fulfilment of this vitally important role necessitated one of the miracles of God, by bringing, *'light out of darkness.'* (Calvin)

It is a paradox of divine power, for the LORD to choose the poorest and weakest sinners in the eyes of the world, to build them up to serve him, so that none can boast of their own worthiness (Jas. 2:5)! There are many examples of this throughout the Bible, none more humble than Amos who claimed to be neither a prophet, nor a prophet's son, but a shepherd.

"But the LORD took me from tending the flock
and said to me,
Go, prophesy to my people!"
(Am. 7:15)

Later Amos prophesied the destruction and also the restoration of Israel!

2. The Tabernacle and Sanctuary (Ex. 26:1–37)
God fulfilled his plan by commanding the Levites to build and furnish a tent, or temporary tabernacle, exactly to the pattern shown to Moses on Mount Sinai, the Holy Mountain (Ex. 25:8). This was declared later to be a copy and shadow of the heavenly Sanctuary (Heb. 8:5). In the very centre of the structure, there was an isolated sanctuary for the most holy presence of the LORD to dwell among his people and at the same time preserve his undefiled estate. This sanctuary was made up of inner and outer rooms, the latter being separated by an outer curtain from the surrounding courtyard. The inner room was the Most Holy Place, set apart for the Ark of the Covenant that was to contain the Testimony protected by cherubim. An atonement cover was made of pure gold, symbolising God's forgiving grace (Ex. 25:17). It was to cover the Ark, where the LORD deigned to meet and speak to sanctified representatives of the people in 'the tent of meeting' to give them his divine commands (Ex. 25:22). An inner curtain

separated the Most Holy Place from the larger outer room, called the Holy Place. According to Hebraic tradition, the Mosaic sanctuary was covered with the hides of unicorns, the noblest of all created beasts!

The colouring of the furnishings reflected God's pattern of décor for the Mosaic tabernacle, which was a true reflection of the colour and order of the heavenly Sanctuary. Gold being the purest of all metals was symbolic of the *Messish* or Christ to come, the spotless Lamb of God. Blue being the celestial colour was an indication of the Deity of Christ. Purple being the royal colour proclaimed Jesus' title, 'King of kings and Lord of lords'. Scarlet foreshadowed the blood the Saviour was destined to shed on the cross!

There was only one entrance and exit to the courtyard, a curtained gate to which the Israelites came with their sin-offerings. (Jesus claimed to be the same gate into the eternal Sanctuary, for all to enter and be saved (Jn. 10:9)!

The Israelites were allowed entry into the outer courtyard, but were strictly forbidden to penetrate the outer curtain and enter the sanctuary. The consecrated priests occupied the Holy Place and were provided access to the courtyard. They acted as mediators, sacrificing the offerings received from the people on the altar; for God had commanded Moses that on festive occasions held three times a year,

"No man should appear before me empty-handed."

(Dt. 16:16)

In this way the LORD revealed to his chosen people the desired conditions of true worship. These ritual acts could only be fulfilled in the sanctuary for his most holy presence, where he communed with them through the mediation of the High Priest.

The significance of this three-tier construction was to impose a symbolic approach to a worldly plan of worship. Such a ministry was declared to be according to the pattern of what is in heaven (Ex.25:40; Heb.8:5). Later it was recorded, 'the first covenant had also ordinances of divine service, and a worldly sanctuary,' which implies that the former reflected the pattern of the eternal divine regulations observed in the heavenly Sanctuary (Heb.9:1. K.J.V.).

The LORD provided Moses with the regulations of worship based on the Covenant of Promise. Under the Levitical system it demanded a piacular or expiatory sacrifice (Lev.17:11). This conferred upon the offerer a sense of sin, through an act of contrition and a plea for pardon made in faith. It was the specific ways of appeasing God's wrath against sin, which required the imputation of their wickedness onto a perfect substitute. God specifically prescribed each sacrifice, their meaning being embodied in the Old Covenant. They were written by command of the LORD and ordained for his spiritual relationship with Israel!

3. The Regulations of Mosaic Worship

The pattern given to Moses provided the building plan of the earthly tabernacle and sanctuary that imposed an approach involving three essential steps in the 'former regulations of worship' upon the Israelites. This requirement meant their earthly worship was preordained to become a copy or reflection of the 'ordinances of divine worship' in the heavenly sanctuary. The three steps included:

1. A mandatory plea of expiation, the blotting out of sins, which demanded a full confession and repentance of all intentional and non-intentional sins.
2. It was followed by voluntary burnt offerings to gain forgiveness.
3. Finally, the first two steps led to a communion, through voluntary thanksgiving offerings to attain peace with their Creator God.

N.B. In this section the more relevant features, reflecting Christ's perfect atonement are 'marked by asterisks'

Step 1: Sin-Offering

This was the only essential or mandatory part of the worship.

God's Spirit summoned the Israelites to attend the tabernacle and they were commanded to bring guilt-offerings, to separate themselves from their intended sins and appease God's wrath. It was an act of expiation by imputation, to make atonement with a Holy God (Lev. 4:1-5), and the sacrifice involved a representative (Isa. 53; Ro. 8:3).

But first, they were to wash themselves, before confessing their intentional sins that had incurred the wrath of God* (Ps. 51:7; Isa. 1:18). Presenting their sin-offerings at the door of the tabernacle and by laying their hands on the head of the substitute, they transferred or imputed their sins onto a perfect 'sin or guilt offering'. After this submission, they pleaded for forgiveness and cleansing.

Step 2: Burnt Offering

This was the first voluntary act of Consecration.

It was a confession of their unintentional sins, due to their ignorance of God's will and ways. This set them apart exclusively for the LORD. (Lev. 1:3) They were to bring a perfect male animal without defect that had been secluded from the flock for the previous three days*. It was presented to the priest for sacrifice, the blood being sprinkled on the altar outside the sanctuary* and the residue had to be poured out at the foot of the altar. *

The flesh was to be a Burnt Offering that had to be wholly consumed. The death of the substitute was an acceptable ransom for atonement, an expression of devotion and commitment, or complete surrender to God. It was also an act of substitution, as payment for their sins. It provided an aroma that was pleasing to the LORD, * foreshadowing the perfect whole sacrifice of Christ, who was a fragrant offering (Ro. 8:3. Eph. 5:2), pleasing to God as our acceptable sacrifice (Php. 4:18).

Step 3: Fellowship Offering

This was the second voluntary act of Communion.

It was between the LORD and a sanctified priest who acted as a mediator between the worshipper and his Creator (Lev. 3:16). This was not mandatory, but an invitation to finally present an offering of peace (*shalom* Hebrew), expressing their thankfulness and thanksgiving and to reflect the holiness of the LORD. It was to gain reconciliation from the LORD and communion between him and the worshipper. This was the only sacrifice that could be partly eaten by the worshipper and priest, as part of a communal meal at a main festival.

This Pattern of Worship was observed every year at the three Great Feasts: Passover, Pentecost and Tabernacles.

4. Yom Kippur

(The Day of Atonement)

"This is to be a lasting ordinance."

(Lev. 16:1–34)

This was a command founded on a sacrificial system specifically prescribed by God, instructing the Israelites in holiness or sanctification. It was to be observed annually on the tenth day of the seventh month (Tishri) of the Sabbath year. The solemn rite of washing before sacrificing was an act of purification by faith. On the Day, three holy and vital stages were observed, as follows:

A Pre-sacrificial Ritual

1. The Sanctification of the High Priest. A young bullock was provided for the High Priest who offered the sacrificial blood to sanctify himself and the sanctuary by sprinkling.* Cleansing of the contents of the sanctuary included the atonement cover on the mercy seat.
2. The selection of the sacrificial lambs and isolation from the flock.* This was to ensure that they were not only without blemish, but also free from infection.

The Sacrificial Ritual

1. A sacrificial lamb was chosen for the LORD, its blood being shed for a ransom to pay the price for the sins of God's people.* The High Priest carried the undefiled blood to the Most Holy Place. It was conveyed in cleansed silver or bronze vessels, to prevent soiling and clotting,* to be sprinkled onto the cover of the mercy seat of the Ark.

2. A live lamb was used as a sin-bearing scapegoat, on which the High Priest imputed vicariously the sins of the Israelites, by the 'laying on of hands'. This was before sending the animal into the desert to carry their sins away, to conciliate or appease the LORD.*

A Post-sacrificial Ritual

1. Any residual sacrificial blood was to be poured out at the base of the altar.*
2. The remnants of the sacrificial animals were to be taken outside the camp* and burned up.

This was an act of substitutional expiation, blotting out their confessed wickedness and rebellion against the commandments of God.

The Sacrifice

The Sacrificial commands made by God were founded on three basic doctrines:

a. The vitality of any animal, including the human race, is in its blood.*
b. The consequence of sin is death; our Creator cannot tolerate any personal erosion of righteousness through human guilt.
c. The only way of salvation is through substitutional atonement, by the imputation or transfer of guilt onto a perfect substitute.*

5. The History of Levitical Doctrine

Following the death of Moses and Joshua's entry into the promised land of Canaan, sacrificial worship continued to be practised. It was extended throughout the rule of the Judges for almost 400 years, followed by another 400 years for the duration of the United and Divided Kingdoms, as follows:

King Saul

During his reign, Samuel advised the king to heed the LORD's command,

> ***"to obey is better than sacrifice, and to hearken than the fat of rams –"***
>
> ***(1 Sam. 15:22)***

King David

He appeared fully aware of this previous warning, as he said later in his writings,

> ***"Sacrifice and offerings thou didst not desire;***
> ***mine ears thou hast opened:***
> ***burnt offerings and sin offerings hast thou not required."***
>
> ***(Ps. 40:6)***

But later, when the prophet Nathan came to chastise the king, after he had committed adultery with Bathsheba, David wrote again,

> ***"Purge me with hyssop, and I shall be clean;***
> ***wash me, and I shall be whiter than snow –***
> ***Then shalt thou be pleased with the sacrifices of righteousness, with burnt offering and whole burnt offering: then shall they offer bullocks upon thine altar."***
>
> ***(Ps. 51:7 and 19)***

After another act of disobedience, the angel of the LORD ordered Gad the prophet to instruct David to build an altar on the site of the threshing floor owned by Araunah the Jebusite, so that he might prevail upon the LORD to stop the plague and the angel sent to destroy Jerusalem. When he had purchased the site, David built an altar to sacrifice burnt offerings and fellowship offerings.

"He called on the LORD, and the LORD answered him with fire from heaven on the altar of burnt offering"
(1 Ch. 21:18–26)

Jerusalem was saved from God's wrath and David retained the favour of his LORD, regardless of his occasional failings. His son Solomon was chosen to succeed him on the throne of Israel! Later David was instructed to charge Solomon to build a house or temple for the 'Name of the LORD' on the same site as his altar.

King Solomon

Traditionally, Solomon built his temple on Mount Moriah in Jerusalem and this appears to be confirmed in Scripture (2 Ch. 3:1). After the completion of the temple for the LORD, Solomon sacrificed thousands of cattle, sheep and goats. Then the king and the people dedicated the temple to God (2 Ch. 7:1–11).

Later, Solomon recorded,

"Every way of man is right in his own eyes:
but the LORD pondereth the hearts.
To do justice and judgement
Is more acceptable to the LORD than sacrifice."
(Pr. 21:2–3 K.J.V.)

King Ahab

During the reign of this evil sovereign, Elijah the prophet built his altar on Mount Carmel. And when he called on the LORD, fire fell and burned up the drenched sacrifice, the wood, the stones and the soil and also licked up the water in the surrounding trench (1 Ki. 18:38). Subsequently, the Mosaic or Levitical rites of sacrifice continued to be practised up to the time of the captivity.

Babylonian captivity

During this period of enslavement, sacrificial worship had to be suspended. Daniel prophesied that long after the rebuilding of Jerusalem and the temple, the Anointed One would appear and be put to death. But later, after the destruction of Jerusalem by another ruler, Daniel prophesied,

"He will confirm a covenant with many – and will put an end to sacrifice and offering."
(Da. 9:26 and 27)

Post-captivity

Despite all the above prophecies, when in 538 B.C. Cyrus king of Persia proclaimed the end of the Babylonian captivity and allowed the exiles return to Jerusalem, Josiah and Zerubbabel began the building of an altar to the God of Israel, to sacrifice burnt offerings on it,

"In accordance with what is written in the Law of Moses, the man of God."

(Ezr. 3:2)

Sacrificial worship continued until 166 B.C. when the Hasmonean dynasty attempted to put an end to Jewish religious observances. Yet it survived, even after the time of the Roman invasion in 63 B.C., when Pompey desecrated the temple by entering the Most Holy Place. Later, Herod restored Zerubbabel's temple in 20 B.C. and revived the Mosaic sacrificial system. Even after Christ's death, it continued to be practised until 70 A.D. when Titus razed the walls of the city to the ground and the temple was finally destroyed for the last time.

6. Sacrificial Atonement

Introduction

In 1534 William Tyndale published his personal translation of the New Testament from old Greek and Hebrew texts into everyday English, in which he believed even a ploughboy would understand. In his text, a Middle English word 'atomen' meaning 'to be reconciled' was given a theological significance for the first time. In his translations of the two old Hebrew words, *kipper* (to repay sin) and *kippur* (the repayment of sin) Tyndale substituted the verb and noun forms with 'atone' and 'atonement' respectively. The latter was used to convey God's divine act of grace, of being 'at one with God', in other words 'reconciliation with God'. The same Hebrew words were translated as 'ransom' in the Septuagint (150 B.C.), a transliteration from the old Greek text. Still later, in 382 A.D., Jerome in his Latin Vulgate Bible translated *kippur* into the Latin noun that is transliterated as 'propitiation'. Jerome also provided the word 'redemption', which was derived from the Latin word *redimere,* meaning to buy back!

Yet, the word atonement appeared only once in Tyndale's New Testament, as in,

"We also joy in God by the means of our Lord Jesus Christ, by whom we have received the atonement."

(Ro. 5:11)

After Tyndale's premature death from martyrdom in 1536, his friend and colleague Myles Coverdale published a complete English Bible. This included all of Tyndale's translations from not only the New, but also the Old Testament including the books from Exodus to Numbers. In these texts the same word 'atonement' was used in preference to 'propitiation'. The greater part of these translations was included in subsequent publication of Henry VIII's 'Great English Bible'. They were later printed in the King James Bible and the Authorised Version, published in 1611, which replaced previous English translations of the Vulgate in the churches.

In more recent N.I.V. Bibles, the same noun 'atonement' is substituted with the word 'reconciliation'! But in this presentation, the medieval words atone and atonement are used for the old Hebrew words in both Old and New Testaments, in deference to William Tyndale's contribution to English literature.

7. The Scroll of the Law *(Sepher Torah)*

The Mosaic Law was contained in a continuous scroll, consisting of the first five books of the Bible. This Scroll was founded on the Ten Commandments, originally written by the finger of the LORD on stone tablets; these were handed to Moses on Mount Sinai, the Mountain of the LORD God. They were the first declarations of faith, clarified and amplified by Moses in his laws for the Israelites to hear and obey.

They also heralded the introduction of a new concept, in which God condescended by grace to accept substitutional atonement by imputation, the blotting out of the sins of his people. This involved the transfer of sin onto a perfect substitute, or scapegoat, symbolically representing a sinner's confessional repentance for its acceptance in the sight of God. Within the divine instructions, Moses included in the Old Testament Law the declaration that every person and everything in the tabernacle be cleansed with sacrificial blood by placing, sprinkling or pouring it upon the people. For by the shedding of innocent blood, ceremonial defilement was removed through this ritual of expiatory sacrifice (Ex.29:21; Lev.8:15).

The blood of an animal is its life, because the vitality of the physical body is dependent upon the circulation of pure blood. If deprived of this source of energy and nutrition, the vital organs (especially the brain) cannot survive and death ensues. Therefore, when shed sacrificially, the blood was considered to symbolise the very essence of the life of the victim. This meant it was to be treated with great respect, since all life was considered sacred! The blood from a sacrificial animal made the act of atonement complete and for this reason alone, every sacrifice included the shedding of blood on the altar within the tabernacle. Man's atonement with God involved the substitution of a life for a life,

"And without the shedding of blood, there is no forgiveness."*

(Lev. 17:11; Heb. 9:22)

Through the Mosaic-Levitical institution, God conveyed a meaningful understanding to his people, which had spiritual import that was specifically prescribed in every sacrifice. Every item received a special meaning in the Old Covenant. Each command was conveyed from God to his chosen people, whose gifts symbolised their devotion and desire for communion with him.

"We are indebted to the Jewish people who preserved and gave us God's written word and of whom also came God's Word made flesh."

(Bill Medcalf)

The practice of the Mosaic Law in the Levitical system developed throughout the ages from early Israelite times. It passed through the Prophetic period and finally entered into the established Levitical Law. The Burnt Offering was the oldest of all the sacrifices being expiatory, in other words it conveyed the blotting out of sin. The restoration of the broken bond between God and man was attained by way of the vicarious transfer of man's guilt onto an innocent victim, which had been selected from a flock and isolated for three days.

The sacrifice involved a representative intermediary

victim or substitute that ransomed the offerer from death. This piacular concept embraced the belief that,

1. There was no sacrifice, which did not convey the idea of a ransom.
2. It required a substitution of a state of guilt, to attain the reconciliation with a Holy God, through the expiation of human guilt.
3. The sprinkling of blood and the burning of sacrificial flesh (Lev. 1:4) were aimed at appeasing the offended Deity (Lev. 17:11).

8. Conclusions

We live in a real world, created by God for people who choose to love and please him. Selfishness and self-centredness have only temporal awards, 'destined to perish' (Col. 2:22). When the Israelites had reached the Promised Land, Moses declared the two alternatives:

"I set before you today life and prosperity, death and destruction – to love the LORD your God and walk in his ways and keep his commands and laws; then you will live and increase, and the Lord your God will bless you – but if your heart turns away and you are not obedient, you will certainly be destroyed!"

(Dt. 30:15–18)

These words were later reiterated in reverse order by St. Paul in his letter to the Roman Church (Ro. 8:13–14).

God has been described as the potter and his creation to clay (Isa. 64:8–9). We cannot disclaim the fact that he made us, nor can we question his decision concerning our make-up and future (Isa. 29:16; 45:9). God is Holy; he has decreed that wickedness is not to be tolerated by those who love him and seek his presence. Therefore he has commanded that men and women must strive to be holy, if they wish to be his people (Lev. 11:44). According to God's Law, sin is death (Ge. 2:17; Ro. 6:1–23), an eternal death, or being excluded from God's very presence in this world and throughout eternity.

The Mosaic Law

But because of the wickedness in the hearts of men and women being inherent, even in those who love him, God decreed that this sentence of death might be imputed. This meant sin being transferred onto a perfect substitute, following the confession and repentance of the guilty person.

God foreknew the cost of the ransom and was prepared to pay the price of our redemption, by imputing our sins upon his only Son, who was the perfect sacrifice (1 Pe. 2:24). To declare the divine cost, God ordained every detail of the Mosaic sacrificial atonement, before the foundations of this created world were laid. In retrospect, they were intended to be a shadow or reflection pointing towards the atoning sacrifice that was to be portrayed at Golgotha. Therefore, without a true understanding of the Mosaic Law, one cannot fully appreciate the content of the cup of sorrow, which our Saviour drank to the very last drop (Mt. 26:42)!

It is interesting to note that Solomon's temple was built in 965 B.C., with three major divisions:

1. The porticus (*'ulam)* or the Temple Courts.
2. The House proper *(hekal)* or the Sanctuary.
3. The Holy of Holies *(debir)* or the Most Holy Place.

The plan was an exact replica of the original house of God, the tabernacle built by human hands!

This same plan was replicated in the rebuilding of Zerubbabel's temple in about 536 B.C. and was retained in the development carried out by Herod in 19 B.C., even if on a grander scale.

Therefore the three-stage pattern of Hebraic worship was upheld until the destruction of the temple in 70 A.D. Thus the same former regulations of worship, the Hebraic liturgy, continued for almost 2,000 years, from 1440 B.C. to 70 A.D. except for the fifty years of exile in Babylon!

Some authorities have labelled Mosaic-Levitical Laws to be 'abattoir theology', revealing their lack of understanding of the doctrine of sacrificial worship. Even some modern theologians are also tending to minimise the theological significance of the shedding of sacrificial blood, by proposing it to be symbolic, or an allegorical representation of the flow of the love and compassion required to fulfil the atoning sacrifice of our Saviour. Yet the sacrificial blood of the Old and New Covenants occupies the central point of Christian belief. This essence of Christian faith is displayed in the divine ordinances included in the communion service, as described in the Synoptic Gospels (Mt. 26; Mk. 14; and Lk. 22; *see also* 1 Cor. 11:23–26).

So let us study the mysteries revealed under the old Mosaic covenant, the salient features being summarised in the following chapter on Hebrew Faith. By recognising these historical truths, we may fully comprehend the divine manifestations of the New Covenant proclaimed by Jesus Christ, the one and only (the only begotten) Son of our heavenly Father (Jn. 1:14).

CHAPTER 3

HEBREW FAITH and EXPECTATIONS

1. Introduction

The human concept of a most holy and powerful Creator God, who reigns eternally in his heaven, slowly dawned upon our early ancestors from the beginning of time. But it was God's divine prerogative to choose a remnant of the human race to be his chosen people. He spoke to them through his prophets who revealed his divine Commandments, Laws and Covenants. From this collection of Scriptural knowledge, the people inherited a simple belief based on his regulations for holy worship. Therefore God's chosen people were provided with a Hebrew faith, which was deep-rooted and founded upon spiritual enlightenment and a confident belief in the truth.

History

It was two thousand years before the birth of Christ, when Abram the Hebrew returned from his triumphant battles with Kedorlaomer and his allies. Melchizedek, the king of Salem, welcomed him and offered refreshments of bread and wine, saying,

"Blessed be Abram of the most high God,
possessor of heaven and earth.
And blessed be the most high God,
which hath delivered thine enemies into thy
hand."

(Ge. 14:17-20. K.J.V.)

This was the first time a man was called a Hebrew and the first Scriptural reference to bread! Abram's name meant 'exalted father' and Melchizedek's name was also from a Hebrew word, '*malki-sedeq*' meaning 'my king of righteousness'. His Most High God had appointed him to be king of Salem, which entitled him 'king of peace' (*shalom*). The title of an ancient king also gained him the recognition of being a great priest of God Most High (Ge. 14:18).

Ancient Hebraic tradition claimed that Melchizedek was, '*none other than Shem, the son of Noah, who founded the City of Peace and reigned in righteousness, being a priest of the Most High God, the founder of the city of a great King*' (*The Land of the Book*, p.695). Shem was upright and righteous like his father, Noah, who considered him destined to be God's chosen servant over his brothers. He and his son, Arphaxad, appear in the genealogy of Jesus, (Lk. 3:23–37) whereas King Melchizedek was later said to be without trace of a human father or mother and without genealogy, without beginning of days or end of life, and like the Son of God he remains a priest for ever (Heb. 7:3).

Shem lived for six hundred years; therefore if Melchizedek was Shem, he would have been four hundred years old when Abram first met him (Ge. 14:17–20)! Perhaps his age accounted for the confusion concerning his birth and death!

Abram was aware of King Melchizedek's religious superiority and gave a tenth of everything he had recovered from his enemies, signifying the recognition of his ancestry and highest order of ancient priesthood. Later, it was said that King David his descendent had been granted the title of heir to the Melchizedek priesthood!

Today, a bronze plaque depicting Melchizedek greeting Abram stands close to King David's citadel on Mount Zion, near the historic 'Joppa (Jaffa) Gate' in Jerusalem. This gate had previously been called in Arabic, the 'Gate of the Friend'. This was in honour of Abram, a friend of God (Jas. 2:23). According to Hebraic tradition the historic meeting took place at this very site! It is salutary to remember that two thousand years later, the same was called the 'Corner Gate' located between King David's original North wall and King Herod's West wall of the old city. It was even later called the 'Garden Gate' (Jn. 19:41), through which a more revered person, also entitled 'A King-Priest for Ever', carried his cross to the quarry called Golgotha; the latter was outside the walls of the old city, above the entrance to Melchizedek's cave!

In modern Hebrew faith, Melchizedek remains a revered religious figure. Josephus acclaimed him to be the founder of Salem (Jerusalem). His God Most High had ordained him to inaugurate and establish an ancient Priesthood, which God the Father had destined to be for his only Son. Therefore this ancient King-Priest, Melchizedek, was and still remains an iconic figure! Surely this divine Priesthood must in the future become instrumental in providing a divine reconciliation between the Hebrew and Christian faiths, through God's promise and good grace (Ge. 9:27; Eph. 2:14–18)!

The fulfilment of God's promise to his people depended upon their obedience to the Ten Commandments, which were inscribed by the finger of God on the two tablets of stone presented to Moses on Mount Horeb (Sinai) (Ex. 31:18; Dt. 9:10). They were referred to as the Testimony or Covenant Law and the LORD commanded Moses to place them in the Ark (Ex. 25:16); whereas the Covenant Book (Ex. 24:7) was recorded in Scripture (Ex. 20:22–23:19). It reveals that the LORD spoke to Moses saying,

> ***"Do not make any gods to be alongside me;***
> ***do not make yourselves gods of silver or gods of gold."***
>
> ***(Ex. 20:23)***

Subsequently, the foundation of Hebrew faith and reverence in the worship of Jehovah were based on three fundamental beliefs, as follows:

i. 'The Scroll of the Law', which was written by hand in Hebrew on animal skins. It contained the Pentateuch (the first five books of the Old Testament) including the ordinances or commands of the LORD. The Hebrews believed it to be provided by the divine ministry of the holy ones or angels and was binding (Dt. 31:9–13, Ps. 89:7 and Heb. 2:2). It is still read with a *Yad*, (a hand or pointer) to revere and protect the written word of God from disfigurement!

ii. Their saviour was Moses, who was their greatest deliverer, prophet and mediator through whom God spoke to them.
iii. Their chosen mediators were the High Priests; they, with the Levitical priesthood, practised the 'former regulations of worship' in the tabernacle and later the temple.

2. The High Priest

This man was a greatly respected and powerful person, chosen by the LORD from the Levite tribe. The very need for such an appointment intimated to the Israelites the wrath of God towards his sinful people. Their original offence was incurred by the deceitful and wilful disobedience of Adam and Eve, committed at the very dawn of creation and imputed upon their progeny. Thereafter, the LORD subsequently refrained from having any direct dealings with the majority of men and women. Yet, after being persuaded by Moses not to destroy the Israelites for their unfaithfulness in the desert, the LORD was inclined to reveal his compassion towards his people. But the reconciliation imposed two conditions: the first being the imputation of their sins upon vicarious sacrifices and the second was divine intercession. The latter had to be through the mediation of a chosen and consecrated people's representative, originally Moses and later the High Priests!

Moses' older brother, Aaron, was the first to be chosen by God, to be anointed and sanctified for the role of High Priest and mediator between the people and the most holy presence of *Yahweh*. His sons were to serve in the tabernacle and support him. Aaron wore the breast piece for making far-reaching decisions at times of crises, casting semi-precious engraved stones as lots. The Urim (curses) indicated a negative response, whereas the Thummim (perfection) represented approval from the covenant LORD (Ex.28:30. *see* TNIV fn.).

Aaron and Moses were members of an elite clan of the Levite tribe, which according to the Mosaic Law would provide future sons to be chosen for consecration as priests.

As the selected High Priest was not without sin, he had to be cleansed by the same process of imputation before he could be presented on the Day of Atonement. His duty was to make intercession at the Seat of Mercy in the Most Holy Place of the Sanctuary, and so gain divine reconciliation for the people. This was God's chosen regulation or channel of worship.

Therefore, to sum up, the High Priest was appointed to be the mediator between the LORD and the Israelites or Hebrew race. He was the first-born son of a priest and possessed a human nature that enabled him to sympathise with those he served. He was from an elite sect of the Levite tribe, an anointed priest, chosen and sanctified by the LORD. There was a chronological limitation to his tenure of office, from thirty years of age when first appointed to fifty years old at retirement. Therefore his priesthood was limited to no more than twenty years. Although being a very pious man, he had inherited a sinful nature from his birth. This had to be imputed upon a near perfect male animal that had been excluded from the herd for three days. This substitute was sacrificed before the High Priest could be anointed; for there was no forgiveness of sin except through the shedding of blood for his atonement.

The Aaronical order of Levitical Priesthood continued for more than a thousand years, from the time that Aaron was anointed by his brother Moses in approximately 1400 B.C., until forty years after the destruction of Herod's temple in 70 A.D.

3. Prophets and Prophecies

Hebrew prophets were divinely commissioned and respected persons, possessing charismatic spiritual powers. They were enabled to interpret the counsels of the Most High God on the day-to-day living of the people. They did not acquire any instruction in prophecy from men, but received their wisdom and calling from God (Jer. 23:22). Their utterances were not considered predictive at the time, as they simply reasoned with the people, '*of righteousness, temperance and judgement to come, as well as the ultimate triumph of the divine purpose among the nations.*' (John Brown.)

In retrospect, however, the Hebrew prophets had a unique faculty of divine foresight, anticipating future events more as warnings rather than fulfilment. Their prophecies often appear to have a double telescopic vision, as many seemed to have been stimulated by an impending occasion.

Yet they also heralded more distant and unforeseeable events, which were not anticipated at the time of conception! Therefore, in retrospect, many Old Testament prophecies appear to have emanated from a supernatural vision or power, having subsequently remained unsurpassed in human history. It has been said that all Hebrew prophecies were Messianic, as they pointed towards the advent of the Anointed One and his work, as saviour of the Jewish nation.

The literary prophets appeared at critical periods in the history of the Hebrew race, as follows:

Primeval period – Jacob and Noah.
Sinaitic period – Moses.
Judges period – Samuel.
United Kingdom period – David, Nathan and Solomon.
Divided Kingdom period – Elijah, Elisha, Jonah, Amos and Hosea.
Assyrian period – Micah, Isaiah and Nahum.
Babylonian period – Jeremiah, Obadiah, Ezekiel and Daniel.
Persian period – Haggai, Zechariah, Malachi, Joel, Obadiah and Jonah.

Conclusions

Whereas John the Baptist was thought by many to be the last of the Hebrew prophets (Mt. 11:9,10)! Moses was considered to be the first and probably the greatest prophet. He freed the Israelites from their yoke of Egyptian slavery and became their only prophetic mediator. On Mount Sinai, he braved the awesome presence of the LORD to plead for the forgiveness of their unfaithfulness. He also instructed them in their worship and led them to the Promised Land, before confronting them with the fact that he was unable to continue to be their saviour, prophet and redeemer! Finally he promised that their God would provide a successor, a prophet like him from amongst them, who would speak concerning the LORD's words and commands (Dt. 18:17–19). The Levitical authority remained unchanged from the earliest days of Hebrew faith. Malachi prophesied the conclusion of the Mosaic Revelation and the arrival of the messenger of a New Covenant; this was followed by 400 years of silence, before the advent of Christ.

4. God's Holy Presence

It has already been inferred that all three divine members of the Holy Trinity existed before the creation of the world and were deeply involved in both its beginning and development. Scripture also reveals that the Sovereign LORD, Son of God, and the Spirit of God appeared in natural and unnatural forms in type teachings. This was before the incarnation of the Messiah or the Christ of the New Testament. Retrospectively, their identification as God's holy presence can be read into Old Testament typologies and theophanies.

God spoke to his prophets through the manifestation of two divine attributes, his wisdom and word. Reference has been made to God's spoken word in the instructions given to Abram and Moses. In the Book of Proverbs, the Wisdom of God is personified and 'linked' to the Word of God in being the firstborn of the LORD and assisting in the creation of the world, as "the craftsman at his side" (Pr. 8:22–30; *see* page 150, the Word of God).

5. The Spirit of God

From the time of the Exodus out of slavery, Moses instructed the Israelites that there was only one LORD God who revealed himself in various ways. They believed him to be God the Creator and the Covenant LORD, whose awesome presence led them through the Sinai desert towards the Promised Land. They also believed the Spirit of *Yahweh* to be God's divine power in action, as revealed in his awesome and fearful breath (*ruah*) and in the wisdom expressed by his word (*dubar*). Whereas God created the universe and all who have lived within, his Spirit sustained all creation by directing its natural development and shaping man's history. The Spirit of God revealed his truth through the inspiration of the prophets, priests and kings, all of whom were selected and became charismatic people (Eze. 2:1–4).

The Old Testament monotheistic belief ruled out any recognition of the Spirit of God being a divine Person. They neither considered him, nor their long awaited Anointed One to be part of God's deity, as the doctrine of the Trinity had not been revealed to them. But it is said that there are four hundred referrals and revelations to the presence of God's Spirit throughout the Old Testament, especially in the prophesies of those who stood in a peculiarly close relationship to God's most holy presence. Yet there were only two references to the Holy Spirit, the first being found in the prayer of David (Ps. 51:11) and the second in Isaiah (Isa. 63:10).

The Holy Spirit revealed God's commands and word to the following prophetic spokesmen – Noah, Abraham, Isaac and Jacob, Moses, Samuel, David, Isaiah, Jeremiah, Ezekiel, Daniel, Micah and many others. Some of these revelations are as follows:

History

Noah

When the LORD saw how great man's wickedness on earth had become, he said,

> ***"My Spirit will not contend with man forever, for he is mortal, his days will be a hundred and twenty years."***
>
> ***(Ge. 6:3)***

But Noah found favour in God's sight, being the first man in Scripture to be called righteous,

"Blameless among the people of his time, and he walked with God.
He did everything just as God commanded him."
(Ge. 6:9 and 22)

Therefore, it is right to assume that the Spirit of God rested upon Noah. At the end of his confinement in the Ark, he sent out a dove and it returned with a freshly plucked olive leaf in its beak (Ge. 8:11). Subsequently, the dove and the olive leaf have become emblematic of the presence and peace of the Holy Spirit.

It is awesome to recall that John the Baptist gave this testimony on one of Noah's descendants,

"I saw the Spirit come down from heaven as a dove and remain on him, the Son of God."
(Jn. 1:32-34)

Abraham

Abram (exalted father) was a descendant of Noah, chosen by God to become the father of a great nation. Because of his faith in the trustworthiness of God, he was promised that all peoples on earth would be blessed through him

"Abram believed the LORD and he credited it to him as righteousness."
(Ge. 15:6)

Later God marked him as his servant and called him by a new name, Abraham (father of many). It was promised that he would not only become the father of many nations, but also Isaac his son and his descendants would be blessed with an everlasting covenant.

As one of his descendants was Jesus of Nazareth, it is rightly assumed that the Spirit of God rested on Abraham, Isaac, Jacob and all their descendants found in the genealogy of Mary's firstborn son (Mt. 1:2–16).

Moses

It has been said, whereas Abraham is considered to be the father of the Hebrews, Moses stands out as their greatest prophet and leader. Moses first met the angel of the LORD, the Spirit of God, when he appeared and spoke to him from flames of fire in a bush near Horeb (Sinai) the mountain of God (Ex. 3:1–3). The Holy Spirit was often accompanied by fire, symbolising the presence of God (Ge. 15:17)! When the Israelites crossed the Red Sea, the Spirit of the LORD went ahead of them in a pillar of cloud by day and a pillar of fire by night to give them light. (Ex. 13:21) Later, outside the tent of meeting, the Spirit appeared in a pillar of cloud (Nu. 12:5; Ps. 99:7).

All these references are clear Scriptural evidence of Moses being constantly aware of the leadership and influence of the Spirit of God, as a divine power. Yet none is more overt compared to his command to the Israelites at the renewal of the Mosaic Covenant,

"Now what I am commanding you today is not too difficult or beyond your reach.
No, the word is very near you; it is in your mouth and in your heart so you may obey it."
(Dt. 30:11–14)

N.B. this may be considered to be a hidden reference to New Testament doctrine, as Paul believed that the word of God was the sword of the Spirit (Eph. 6:17).

Judges of Israel

The Book of Judges includes a series of six leaders chosen to judge and govern the Israelites after the death of Joshua, each one being blessed by the Spirit of the LORD. They included Gideon (Jdg. 6:34) Jephthah (Jdg. 11:29) and Samson (Jdg. 13:25). Towards the end of this period, lasting over 350 years, Samuel was born and grew up to be acknowledged as an attested prophet of the LORD. He was instructed by God to anoint Saul as a ruler and king. Later the Spirit of God came on Saul, in power. After prophesising he was changed into a different person (1 Sam. 10:1- 11). But Saul disobeyed the LORD and was rejected, the Spirit of the LORD having departed from him.

Samuel and David

When Samuel was a boy (12 years old, according to Josephus) the word of the LORD called him and remained with him, as he grew up to be attested as a prophet (1 Sam. 3:1–21).

Later he was commanded by the LORD to travel to Bethlehem and consecrate Jesse and his sons, one of whom he was to anoint as king. Yet the LORD did not look at their outward appearance, but at their hearts – rejecting seven of them. Eventually they sent for David, the youngest son, and the LORD chose him. So Samuel took the horn, filled with the oil of joy and anointed him. From that day the Spirit of the LORD came on David in power (1 Sam. 16:13).

Isaiah made five important references to God's Spirit, three concerning his outpouring (Isa.32:15, 44:3, 59:21). Whereas **Ezekiel** refers to the abundant blessings on Israel through the Spirit (Eze.36:26–27, 39:29). And **Joel** refers to the outpouring of God's Spirit on the Day of the LORD (Joel2:28–29). Finally, **Zechariah** in his prophetic vision recorded the words of the LORD Almighty, in reference to Zerubbabel's rebuilding of the temple in Jerusalem:

"Not by might nor by power, but by my Spirit."
(Zec.4:6)

Conclusions

It is not intended for this to be a comprehensive list of symbolic references to the acknowledgement of the existence of the gracious Spirit, as a divine power related to the Covenant LORD in the Old Testament. But apart from the two references given, there is little to suggest further acknowledgement of the Spirit of God being anything other than a manifestation of God, rather than a holy person who should be worshipped as a divine member of the Godhead. At that stage, the doctrine of the Holy Trinity had not been revealed for them to recognise his personality!

In retrospect, this appears to be vital evidence of God's unfolding plan of his redemptive love! Yet it has been said, with the knowledge acquired from the New Testament, it is possible to retrospectively read into the Old Testament the Holy Spirit's distinct personality appearing as a divine influence. Therefore in both Testaments, the Holy Spirit appears as a unique source of grace that transforms a believer through repentance and faith.

6. The Anointed One, Son of God, Son of Man

The Hebrews did not use the title 'Messiah' for the saviour whose advent they eagerly awaited, as in their historic literature the word was a transliteration of the Hebrew word '*mashiah*', an adjective used to describe any person who had been divinely anointed by the LORD. Therefore it had no greater significance; and so in preference, in their longed-for anticipations, they chose the title of 'The Anointed One' for their God-sent deliverer.

Their prophets and priests taught them to believe the Anointed One would be like Moses, a unique leader of his priesthood and saviour of his people. But he would belong to the royal tribe of Judah that had never served the LORD at the altar (Ex. 29:44), whereas the Mosaic Law had confined this privilege to the priesthood of Aaron, his sons and their descendants, all of whom were elite members of the Levitical tribe. Therefore the advent would of necessity involve a change of priesthood, heralded by a New Covenant with the LORD.

History

There are many references to the Anointed One throughout the Old Testament, but from the earliest times, the following quotes are of more poignant significance.

When Jacob was near to the end of his life, he blessed his twelve sons and prophetically ascribed their future.

On Judah, his father prophesied,

"The sceptre would not pass from the House of Judah, nor the ruler's staff from between his feet, until he to whom it belongs shall come and the obedience of the nations be his."

(Ge. 49:10)

In retrospect, this was probably the first and the earliest promise to the Israelites that a royal person would appear to lead them and become a deliverer and redeemer of their nation.

This Messianic promise was upheld when Balaam prophesied to Balak, king of the Moabites,

"A star will come out of Jacob,
a sceptre will rise out of Israel –
and a ruler will come out of Jacob –"

(Nu. 24:17 and 19)

This Messianic prophecy appeared to be confirmed when King David wrote a prayer of extreme anguish and sorrow, being that expressed by a righteous man who has been persuaded by his sufferings into believing that he has been forsaken,

"My God, my God, why hast thou forsaken me?
Why art thou so far from helping me,
And from the words of my roaring?
O my God, I cry in the daytime,
But thou hearest not –"

(Ps. 22:1–22)

These wonderful words so reverently described the suffering or passion of a crucified Saviour, yet it remains a divine mystery (1 Pet. 1:10–11) for Jesus Christ to have repeated them upon the cross of Golgotha, a thousand years later (Mt. 27:45)! Therefore they must be truly prophetic and Messianic in character.

Later, King David prophesied,

> ***"The LORD said unto my Lord,***
> ***'Sit thou at my right hand,***
> ***until I make thine enemies thy footstool.'***
>
> ***The LORD hath sworn,***
> ***and will not repent,***
> ***Thou art a priest for ever***
> ***after the order of Melchizedek"***
>
> ***(Ps. 110:1–4)***

In this psalm of David, verses one and four contain two oracles that might well be considered to be referring to the coronation enthronement of a future Davidic king! Yet Hebraic tradition recognised their prophetic importance in relation to their long-awaited, anointed King-Priest, long before New Testament writers highlighted their Messianic significance.

It is also significant that they were written about halfway through the duration of the Aaronical priesthood. It was the first indication of the identity of the promised Anointed One, who was to succeed Moses. He was to be a priest of an historic order, other than the tribe of the established Levitical priesthood. Originally, it appeared that the promise would be fulfilled by the Davidic dynasty! (970 B.C.)

But over four hundred years later, in 570 B.C., Ezekiel cast doubt on this Hebraic belief when he condemned Zedekiah. This last prince of Israel was commanded to remove the diadem and take off the crown, as it would not be restored,

"Until he come whose right it is,
and I will give it him."
(Eze. 21:26–27)

Isaiah is considered by many theological scholars to be the pre-eminent prophet of Israel, because of his historical and prophetic writings. Many were eventually believed to be Messianic and were quoted by Jesus and his followers.

"Therefore the LORD himself will give you a sign.
The virgin will be with child and will give birth to a son,
And will call him Immanuel."
which means, 'God with us'!
(Isa. 7:14)

"Land of Zebulun and land of Naphtali
In the future he will honour Galilee of the Gentiles –
The people walking in darkness
Have seen a great light;
On those living in the land of the shadow of death
A light has dawned."
(Isa. 9:1–2)

"For unto us a child is born, unto us a son is given:
and the government shall be upon his shoulder:
and his name shall be called Wonderful,
Counsellor.
The Mighty God, The Everlasting Father, The
Prince of Peace.
Of the increase of his government and peace there
shall be no end"

(*Isa. 9:6–7; see* Mt. 4:15–16)

"And there shall come forth a rod out of the stem of
Jesse,
and a Branch shall grow out of his roots:
And the spirit of the LORD shall rest upon him,
the spirit of wisdom and understanding"

(Isa. 11:1–4)

"The voice of him that crieth in the wilderness,
Prepare ye the way of the LORD,
Make straight in the desert a highway for our God.
Every valley shall be exalted and every mountain
and hill shall be made low;
And the crooked shall be made straight and the
rough places plain:
And the glory of the LORD shall be revealed, and
all flesh shall see it together:
For the mouth of the LORD has spoken"

(Isa. 40:3–5)

The Hebrews at that time and even subsequently have believed this prophecy referred to the journey of a future king to a distant country. Yet John the Baptist, who was considered to be the last of the Old Testament prophets, gave the prophecy its true Messianic significance (Lk. 3:1–6; *see* NIV text reference to Lk. 3:4).

There has been much controversy in the past among Hebraic theologians, as to the true authorship of the book of the words of Isaiah. They believed that the first forty-two chapters were written by the Prophet, but refused to accept the remainder as from the same pen. This misbelief was possibly due to the greater numbers of Messianic prophecies in the later chapters, which proved unacceptable to them. Yet the majority of unbiased authorities accept the true authorship of all the contents.

The Royal Servant of the LORD

"BEHOLD my servant, whom I uphold; mine elect, in whom my soul delighteth;
I have put my spirit upon him: he shall bring forth judgement on the Gentiles.
He shall not cry, nor lift up, nor cause his voice to be heard in the street.
A bruised reed shall he not break; and the smoking flax shall he not quench;
He shall bring forth judgement unto truth –
I the LORD have called thee in righteousness, and will hold thine hand,
And will keep thee, and give thee for a covenant of the people,
For a light unto the Gentiles;
To open the blind eyes, to bring out the prisoners from the prison,
And them who sit in darkness out of the prison house –"

(*Isa. 42:1–7*)

"I gave my back to the smiters, and my cheeks to them that plucked out the hair:
I hid not my face from shame and spitting."
(Isa. 50:6)

The Suffering and Glorified Servant.

"Who hath believed our report? And to whom is the arm of the LORD revealed?
For he shall grow up before him as a tender plant and as a root out of a dry ground:
He shall have no form nor comeliness and when we shall see him,
There is no beauty that we should desire him.
He was despised and rejected of men: a man of sorrow and acquainted with grief:
And we hid as it were our faces from him: he was despised and we esteemed him not.
Surely he hath borne our griefs and carried our sorrows:
Yet we did esteem him stricken of God, and afflicted.
But he was wounded for our transgressions; he was bruised for our iniquities,
The chastisement of our peace was upon him; and with his stripes we are healed.
All we like sheep have gone astray: we have turned everyone to his own way;
And the LORD hath laid upon him the iniquity of us all.
He was oppressed, and he was afflicted, yet he opened not his mouth;

He is brought like a lamb to the slaughter; and
as a sheep before her shearers is dumb,
So he openeth not his mouth.
He was taken from prison and from judgement:
and who shall declare his generation?
For he was cut off from the land of the living;
for the transgression of my people was he
stricken.
And he made his grave with the wicked, and
with the rich in his death:
because he had done no violence, neither was
any deceit in his mouth.
Yet it pleased the LORD to bruise him: he hath
put him to grief:
when thou shalt make his soul an offering for
sin,
he shall see his seed, he shall prolong his days,
and the pleasure of the LORD shall prosper in
his hand.
He shall see the travail of his soul, and shall be
satisfied:
by his knowledge shall my righteous servant
justify many, for he will bare their iniquities.
Therefore I will divide him a portion of the
great, and he shall divide the spoil with the
strong:
Because he has poured out his soul unto death;
And he was numbered with the transgressors;
and he bare the sin of many,
And made intercession for the transgressors".
(Isa. 53:1–12)

Daniel had a vision towards the end of his Babylonian captivity, in which four great beasts came out of the sea and were duly dealt with by the Ancient of Days. The dream concluded with the following scenario,

"I saw in the night visions, and, behold one like the son of man came with the clouds of heaven, and came to the Ancient of Days, and they brought him near before him.
And there was given him dominion, and glory, and a kingdom, that all people, nations and languages, should serve him; his dominion is an everlasting dominion, which shall not pass away, and his kingdom is one that shall not be destroyed."
(Da. 7:13–14)

The 'son of man' was identified later to be the Messiah or the 'Anointed One' who will be put to death (Da. 9:25:26).

Of all the remaining prophecies, there are three more of outstanding importance:

Micah was a contemporary of Isaiah and is believed to have written these words seven hundred years before Jesus was born in Bethlehem!

"But thou, Bethlehem Ephratah,
though thou be little among the thousands of Judah.
Yet out of thee shall he come forth unto me that is to be ruler in Israel,
whose goings forth have been from of old, from everlasting."
(Mic. 5:2)

Haggai prophesied at the rebuilding of the Temple in Jerusalem, after the Babylonian captivity,

"Yet once, it is a little while, and I will shake the heavens and the earth,
and the sea and the dry land. And I will shake all nations'
And the desire of all nations shall come:
And I will fill this house with glory, saith the LORD of hosts."

(*Hag. 2:6 and 7*)

At the same time Zechariah prophesied.

"Rejoice greatly, O daughter of Zion; shout O daughter of Jerusalem;
behold, thy King cometh unto thee: he is just, and having salvation;
lowly, and riding upon an ass, and upon a colt the foal of an ass –
and he shall speak peace unto the heathen,
and his dominion shall be from sea even to sea,
and from the river to the ends of the earth."

(Zec. *9:9–10*)

(The above quotations were chosen from the King James Version, as it was written in a script of high literal standard and in a form more easily memorised than subsequent translations.)

7. Conclusions

Therefore, to sum up the evidence from all the Scriptural truths included in the above quotations, the Israelites and subsequently the Hebrew race were comforted by their prophets with the hope that the LORD would raise up another anointed prophet and King-Priest from among them. He would succeed their forefather Moses in being a national saviour and redeemer, their prophet, priest and king.

The traditional Hebraic promise was that of a future ruler who would unify the nation, as previously accomplished by King David. He would be of the stem of Jesse and the seed of David, to sit upon his throne and rule their kingdom. His reign would be eternal. As a Servant of the LORD, he would inherit the Melchizedek and Davidic titles of Wonderful, Counsellor, Mighty God, Everlasting Father and Prince of Peace. The promise was to be fulfilled in the year of the LORD'S Favour (Isa. 61:2; *see* page 89).

Therefore the anointed King-Priest would be of the family of David, the royal tribe of Judah, which had never qualified previously to be of the old order of priesthood, as it had not served the LORD at the altar (Ex. 29:44). For the Mosaic commands had confined this privilege to the priesthood of Aaron and his sons, and their descendants, all of whom were members of the Levitical tribe. A new order had to be created, to be entirely different from the preceding priesthood that had failed to fulfil God's Law and reach his perfection. The new priesthood would be of the ancient order of Melchizedek and would be superior in dignity compared to its predecessor. This change of priesthood would herald a new Covenant and commands, which meant the old Mosaic Covenant and its orders would be annulled. Yet this new King-Priest would be a firstborn son of a woman, possessing both spiritual and human natures. His being Son of God and Son of Man would enable him to sympathise with the people.

This Levitical ideology had existed for more than a thousand years, during which time it had become 'engraved in stone', as the Mosaic Institution of divine origin. Its introduction had been iconic and was confirmed and ratified by a series of most impressive events. The divine covenants provided great advantages for the Hebrews and subsequently the Jewish race. For they had been given the very word of God (Logos) written in the Scroll of the Law (*Sepher Torah*), which included not only the laws and commandments, but also the divine covenants (Ro. 3:1–4, 9: 4–5) and promises (Isa. 43:1–7, 49:15–18). Their long survival produced not only a powerful influence, but also a '*charm of human ancestry'* (John .Brown.).

All this meant the Hebrews could not accept the Messianic prophecies that foresaw their eagerly awaited Anointed One as a suffering and glorified servant,

"Despised and rejected of men: a man of sorrow and acquainted with grief."

(*Isa. 53:3*)

For they had been promised they would be given a new king. He would be a son of David, all-powerful and conquering, an eternal scourge to the foes of Israel (Nu. 24:17–19).

As their Scribes, Pharisees, and teachers of the Law had a sound knowledge of the Old Covenant, they should have been prepared to persuade the people into accepting this new concept of the *Messish (or Mashiah)*. But even their leaders were blinded from accepting the truth of God, because of the 'veil' that prevented them from seeing what was passing away (2 Cor. 3:13–15). This was not due to personal ignorance, but because they had forsaken the LORD and broken the covenant he had made with them. Therefore the LORD dulled their ears and closed their eyes (Mt. 13:14–15).

As Jesus quoted to his disciples, from Isaiah,

> **"They may be ever seeing but never perceiving,**
> **and ever hearing but never understanding;**
> **otherwise they might turn and be forgiven!"**
> **(*Isa. 6:9–10*; Mk. 4:12.)**

Moses foresaw this calamity before he died, as he was warned that the LORD would turn his back on his people and hide his face from them, because of their wickedness (Dt. 31:16–18).

Even the promises of a new covenant, including forgiveness and the blotting out of their sins, was insufficient to overcome their stubborn refusal of acceptance (Jer. 31:31–37; Eze. 2:3–7). They were warned, however, that the promise was not for their sakes, but for the name of their God (Eze. 36:22–23; Ro. 2:24).

The Hebrew hope was one of becoming members of a privileged Jewish faith, through the new leadership of the Anointed One. This hardened the minds of the majority of orthodox Jews in their opposition to Christian belief and prevented their acceptance of Jesus being the Messiah, or the Christ! Christianity was made even more unpalatable by its avowed purpose of abolishing and replacing the Mosaic Covenant, which in Jewish belief was destined for everlasting endurance. In addition the New Covenant declared

Judaism to be none other than an introductory institution, as it had been proved to be imperfect and confined to a national and temporal belief!

It was Hebraic belief that the advent of the Anointed One would be preceded by the reappearance of the prophet Elijah (Mal. 4:4–5). Even today at Passover each orthodox Jewish family provides an empty chair at their table, to welcome the Prophet when he arrives! They do not accept the later revelation that the birth and ministry of John the Baptist spiritually fulfilled this promise (Mt. 11:14, 17:10–13).

It is interesting to note that whereas the Mosaic Covenant declared,

"Without the shedding of blood, there is no forgiveness."

(Lev. 17:11)

The New Covenant declares that true love (agape) demands sacrifice,

"This is love: not that we loved God, but that he loved us
and sent his Son as an atoning sacrifice for our sins."

(1 Jn. 4:10)

In retrospect, the former demand appears as a reflection in reverse order to the latter declaration!

In comparison to the Old Covenant, Christianity proclaimed itself to be universal, an everlasting dispensation of religious truth and dedication. For under this new order there would be,

"Neither Jew nor Greek, slave nor free, male nor female,
for you are all one in Christ Jesus"
(Gal. 3:28)

There would be no form of racial discrimination, as all believers in the Lord Jesus Christ are meant to worship together in the closest bonds of fellowship and spiritual love in a holy society.

There was none born of a woman other than Jesus Christ whose ancestry, birth, discipline of life, humility and teachings fulfilled the above Messianic prophecies. No more than fifty years following the transfiguration of Jesus in the presence of Peter, James and John, the Apostles recalled they were eyewitnesses of his majesty on the sacred mountain (2 Pe. 1:17–18).

They were terrified when they heard God's voice from heaven; later John witnessed in the prologue of his Gospel,

"We have seen his glory, the glory of the One and Only,
who came from the Father, full of grace and truth.
For the law was given through Moses,
grace and truth came through Jesus Christ."
(Jn. 1:14 and 17)

PART 2

THE NEW TESTAMENT CHRISTIAN WORSHIP

CHAPTER 4

THE ETERNAL COVENANT

1. Introduction

It is apparent from Scripture, God's decision to make human beings in his own image (Ge. 1:27) might well have provided the divinely foreseeable event that man would foolishly follow the fallen angels in their wish to become free from all heavenly regulations (Rev. 12:7–9). Such an achievement would have meant man being capable of deciding what was right or wrong for himself, irrespective of the manifold wisdom and love emanating from his Creator (Heb. 12:9–11). This craving for independence was the nature of original sin, so colourfully symbolised in the creative story of the Garden of Eden. In this worldly paradise, the serpent was able to persuade the woman and man that God's grace was sufficient to countenance the eating of the forbidden and sacred fruit from the 'tree of the knowledge of good and evil' without the fear of divine judgement.

God's holiness and faithfulness are two of his eternal attributes that provide the foundation of his infinite sovereignty and ever-forgiving holy love. The pivotal balance of the divine scales is God's perfect justice, upheld by the power of his Word. This justice was sustained in his commandments and laws spoken to Moses on Mount Sinai (Ex. 20–23) and later inscribed in stone by the finger of God (Ex. 24:12, 31:18). They revealed the hidden secrets of God's holiness, which embraced his mercy or forgiving grace towards repentant believers who love and trust him! Such divine perfection requires sufficient strength and durability to maintain his faithfulness throughout eternity.

Exodus reveals the awesomeness and terror that the LORD's spoken word created in the hearts of the Israelites, when his holy presence descended upon Mount Sinai (Ex. 19:16). Even Moses trembled with fear, the same as did Peter, James and John on the Mount of Transfiguration (Mk. 9:6). Subsequently the Old Testament revealed the LORD's faithfulness, which was displayed in his covenanted love and mercy towards his chosen people.

But Adam's progeny continued to portray an inherent sinfulness and stubborn ignorance that was founded on their pride and arrogance. In his response to Moses' pleading, the LORD not only forgave the rebellious Israelites, but also withheld the punishment they deserved. In addition, they were offered a land flowing with milk and honey! Yet even before the fulfilment of the Promise, the LORD foreknew that his people would rebel again and forsake the holy love revealed to them in the Old Covenant (Dt. 31:14–18). Its failure to captivate the reverence of a sin-torn nation was due entirely to the accruing deceit of its people.

Moses' immediate successor was Joshua, who is retrospectively considered to be an Old Testament type, a prefigurement or foreshadowing of Christ! Although originally named Hoshua (meaning salvation) Moses renamed him Joshua (meaning, the LORD saves, or gives victory).

More than two thousand years later, an angel of the Lord instructed Mary to call her future son Jesus, which is the English transliteration of the Greek word translated from the old Hebrew name Joshua. It has been pointed out previously, whereas Joshua led the LORD's chosen people through all their tribulations in the desert to the Promised Land, Jesus likewise leads his people through their worldly trials to an eternal rest in his paradisiacal kingdom in heaven!

The history of the LORD God's elect, Abraham's spiritual progeny (Gal. 3:29) reveals the truth that our Creator is incapable of breaking the Covenants or Promises he makes with those he has chosen to love. At times, the stupidity shown by this remnant of his creation has driven God to turn away in utter despair (Ps. 28:1–6), but the overwhelming desire to rescue them returns sooner than later. His forgiving grace far outweighs their waywardness. The impending failure of the people's response towards the Old Covenant led to the Messianic Gospel. The fulfilment incurred the anointing of a new King-Priest and also the heralding of a new Promise, a Covenant of Love.

The old Hebrew name for God's love was '*aheb*', but the Septuagint or LXX translation of the Old Testament's 'Song of Songs' introduced the Greek word '*agape*'. Later it was used frequently in the New Testament to describe the never failing love of God, as revealed in Jesus Christ. It is an unselfish and unnatural love, which does not seek its own way (1 Jn. 4:7–19). A*gape* is also a devotional and committable love, self-giving and sacrificial. Such grace '*charis*'arises out of the devotional love of Jesus Christ. This divine love should also be recognisable in all dedicated believers, as it implies the virtue of providing undeserved love that frequently necessitates personal sacrifice. In common grace, God essentially gives himself in Christ, to overcome human helplessness in sin. (Calvin) *Agape* is banished from the hearts of men and women by sin, but is restored by the Holy Spirit through grace to motivate Christian living. Such regeneration renews the believer progressively towards the perfect image of God through the process of sanctification.

The Gospel of the New Testament heralds the promise of God's Word, as was spoken by his prophets in the Old Testament (Ro. 1:1–4) concerning the advent of a new and eternal covenant. It has been previously pointed out that both Testaments are in complete harmony by having no inconsistencies, as both emanated from the same divine source.

It should therefore be of no surprise to find the record of the genealogy of Jesus Christ the son of David, the son of Abraham, to be the first words written by Matthew at the beginning of the New Testament. This is the endorsement of the first words of the Old Testament, "In the beginning God created –" (Ge. 1:1) as enlightened by the Apostle John in the Prologue of his Gospel!

"In the beginning was the Word, and the Word was with God, and the Word was God."

(Jn. 1:1)

2. The Promise

"I will raise up for them a prophet like you from among the people, and will put my words into his mouth. He will tell them everything I command him. I myself will call to account anyone who does not listen to my words that the prophet speaks in my name."

(Dt. 18:17–19)

This divine promise made to Moses on Mount Horeb was included in his farewell address to the Israelites before they entered Canaan, the Promised Land. Like many Old Testament prophesies, the promise was not only for the immediate future following Moses death, as fulfilled by Joshua, but also included more distant and unforeseeable events. It is therefore believed to refer to a later Messianic expectation that received complete fulfilment in the advent of Jesus Christ.

Therefore the New Testament reveals the Promise. The first three books, the Synoptic Gospels, provide the indisputable evidence that Jesus was the Messiah. His whole life and ministry provided the requirements of God's Law, as previously revealed in the Old Testament Scriptures and later quoted repeatedly by the Gospel writers. Such predictions were emphasised in the previous chapters of Part 1 (*see* note on page 37 re. the mark of the asterisk).

The understanding of the relationship between God's Old Covenant Law and the Gospel of Salvation has varied and indeed still varies between the old and modern sects of Christian belief. However, it is generally agreed that God's divine Law is unchangeable and eternal. Its observance has been compared to a sheet of glass, in that even a slight infringement shatters the whole (Jas. 2:10)! History has proved, repeatedly, that we are incapable of fulfilling the perfect standards the Law demands, due to the inherent sin in our hearts. We therefore stand condemned in the sight of God. Under such circumstances, the Gospels contain the good news that Jesus fulfilled the requirements of the Law, by allowing the sins of his people to be imputed upon his sinless body. As a scapegoat, he carried our sins away; as a sacrificial lamb, he died bearing the curse of eternal death inherent in all believers.

Therefore, as a Saviour and Redeemer, he provides

salvation for all who believe in him. This saving grace is received by faith alone and not by good works.

It does not mean that Christians can afford to ignore the Law (for this is antinomianism) as the latter has a positive influence upon a believer's desire to please God in one's day-to-day living.

To sum up, under the Old Covenant God provided his mercy for all repentant believers by imputation and the forgiveness of sins. Under the New Covenant, Christ provides the same forgiving grace through justification by faith, facilitating the same divine process of salvation. God's Holy Spirit completes this work of sanctification, by revealing God's will in his Word and providing the spiritual strength for its fulfilment in response to our spiritual prayers.

3. The Fulfilment of the Promise

Jesus never disguised himself, but from the very beginning of his ministry he set out to reveal his power and authority to those who believed in him. John the Baptist identified Jesus as the Lamb of God and declared him to be God's Chosen One (Jn. 1:34). Andrew was the first of his disciples to recognise Jesus to be the Messiah and brought his brother Peter to him (Jn. 1:40–41). Later, John declared:

> **"For the one whom God has sent speaks the words of God,**
> **for God gives the Spirit without limit."**
> **(Jn. 3:34.)**

When Jesus began his ministry in Nazareth, he was given the Scroll of the Law to read, containing the words of Isaiah's prophecy,

"The Spirit of the Lord is on me,
Because he has anointed me to proclaim the good news to the poor.
He has sent me to proclaim freedom for the prisoners
And recovery of sight for the blind,
To release the oppressed,
To proclaim the year of the Lord's favour."
(Lk. 4:18–19; *see Isa.42:1–7, 61:1–2a*)

Then he sat down to preach and began with the words,

"Today this scripture is fulfilled in your hearing."

And those present were amazed to hear such gracious words from Joseph's son (Lk. 4:22).

Two years later, at the height of his ministry, Jesus confronted his disciples by challenging their belief, with the immortal words,

"Who do you say I am?"
(Mt. 16:15; Mk.8:29; Lk. 9:20)

And it was only after Peter's confession that Jesus began to teach them the doctrine of his death and resurrection (Mt. 16:21). Thus Jesus Christ laid down the fundamental precept; before anyone can begin to comprehend the doctrine of the Cross, it is essential to believe he is the Son of God! Later, Jesus instructed his disciples with the same principles in reverse order by revealing the miraculously healed wounds of his body, as proof of his resurrection, before telling them to stop doubting and believe he was the Messiah. Thomas immediately recognised him to be his risen Lord and his God (Jn. 20:26–28)!

The New Testament doctrine concerning the death and resurrection of the Lord Jesus Christ cannot be fully understood except in the light provided by Old Testament doctrines, especially those concerning the significance of the divine instruction enshrined in the Mosaic instruction on sacrificial worship. As previously stated,

> *'The entire sacrificial ritual is typological preparation pointing towards the character and coming of the Messiah and of salvation in him.' (Hendriksen)*

Therefore, it appears with hindsight that the Levitical sacrifice was a poor reflection in a mirror, or even a distorted image, of the authentic perfect sacrifice that was to come; for as in any mirror, the reflected image appears in reverse order, with regard to the heavenly plan of salvation! The two vital roles of Saviour and Redeemer were fulfilled in the same three sacrificial stages described under the Old Covenant, but Jesus Christ's atonement was sufficient, without need of repetition (*see* Heb. 10:8–10).

The Apostle Paul summed up the doctrine of the Cross,

"For through the law I died to the law so that I might live for God.
I have been crucified with Christ and I no longer live, but Christ lives in me.
The life I live in the body, I live by faith in the Son of God,
Who loved me and gave himself for me."
(Gal. 2:19-20)

CHAPTER 5

THE GOSPEL OF JESUS CHRIST

1. Introduction

The Mosaic instruction included three stages of sacrificial worship. Firstly, the selection and isolation of the sacrificial lamb for three days; this was to ensure that they were without blemish and infection. It was followed by the shedding of its blood for the forgiveness of sins, any excess being poured out at the foot of the altar and covered with soil. Then the sins of the people were laid on a scapegoat, to fulfil the atonement. Yet the failure of this yearly Mosaic ritual to cleanse the people of their wilful disobedience was soon recorded by the psalmist, who said of his LORD,

"Sacrifice and offering you did not desire –"
(*Ps. 40:6–8*)

(These prophetic words of David were quoted later, as being repeated by Christ (Heb. 10:5–7).

Jesus completed his life's redemptive work by first becoming the divine scapegoat and then the sacrificial lamb, followed by three days of entombment in the grave; thus fulfilling his atoning sacrifice. So let us compare Christ's suffering to the previous pattern of Mosaic worship, which was in reverse order to the pre-ordained original sacrifice planned to take place at Golgotha!

2. Christ's Atonement

Stage One

To fulfil his sacrificial atonement, Jesus paid the ransom price for the sins of the world that were vicariously imputed upon his body. Therefore the suffering of Jesus upon the cross of Golgotha was the initial role being that of the scapegoat. It was both vicarious and sacrificial, to fulfil all the demands of God's justice, as previously described in the Old Testament Sacrificial Worship (Lev. 1:1-4). His suffering or passion, was completed before the time of his cry, "It is finished" (Jn. 19:30).

Stage Two

He then became the divine sacrificial lamb by voluntarily laying down his life through the shedding of his precious blood. In so doing, he redeemed all who believe him to be the Son of God. In this role as the sacrificial lamb, he fulfilled the atonement for his chosen people, giving his life as a ransom for many (Mt. 20:28) and procuring their eternal redemption. Towards the end of this stage, the Holy Spirit conveyed his sacrificial blood to 'the seat of mercy' in the paradisiacal sanctuary. This final act was to gain the forgiveness of his imputed sins and so purify himself before paying the ransom for our redemption.

Stage Three

Then his body was entombed for three days before his resurrection, to fulfil the three stages of the atonement.

Jesus Christ's atoning sacrifice was significantly displayed on the cross of Golgotha. It was there that the humility of his incarnation was brought to a climax when he was shamefully stripped of his garments, which according to orthodox Hebrew tradition was the only remaining evidence of his human ancestry. For example, in the parable of the Good Samaritan, the priest passed on the other side of the road, because he could not identify the religion of the naked man (Lk. 10:30–31)! In the words of Hendriksen, Jesus assumed the anonymity of the criminals crucified with him, by embracing the '*curse of nakedness*' (Ge. 3:9-11; 9:20–23).

3. Christ's Sacrifice

Warfield in his study of 'Christ our Sacrifice' stated,

> *'The doctrine of the sacrificial death of Christ (a vicarious sacrifice) is embodied in Christianity, as an essential element of the system; but in a very real sense it constitutes Christianity and differentiates it from other religions.'*

There have been many previous attempts to explain the sudden and unnatural death of Jesus upon the cross (Mk. 15:44) but none have provided an adequate explanation. One of the great mysteries of the crucifixion arose from it being a form of execution that did not cause any obvious fatal loss of blood. The victims usually died from the excruciating pain (Latin, *excruciare, crux,* to torment on the cross) and exhaustion, described by Josephus to be, '*the most wretched way of dying.*'

The lack of Scriptural evidence concerning an overt shedding of Christ's blood was thought to rule out exsanguination being the cause of death. Added to this, any unusual excessive haemorrhaging from Christ's head, hands and feet (as well as from the postmortal spear wound) fell to the ground and was therefore contaminated. This would have excluded its use for atonement, because sacrificial blood had to be pure and undefiled!

Later in his study, Warfield quoted Paul Fiebig's comment,

'Why is this redemption and the forgiveness of sins so often connected to the blood of Jesus? This is remarkable for the death on the cross was not so very bloody that it should be precisely the blood of Jesus, which so impressed the eyewitnesses and the first Christians. This emphasis on the blood cannot be explained therefore from the kind of death that Jesus died!'

But, it is conceivable for the Lord Jesus Christ, towards the end of his passion when his body was bruised and traumatised, to have died from a massive internal haemorrhage into the sterile peritoneal cavity of his abdomen or belly, such as can occur from a traumatic or spontaneous rupture of the spleen. Under these circumstances, there would be no overt evidence of such a fatal blood loss to the untrained observer. Death would have ensued from a fatal drop of blood pressure (syncope) following the loss of one third to half the normal blood volume (five litres) (*see* Wilkinson 2000).

It is hard to conceive another form of sacrifice that would have provided the opportunity to fulfil the essential demands of the sacrificial Law of God! Christ's blood had to remain fluid and sterile for more than three hours, providing the divine opportunity for the major portion of the sacrificial blood to be carried away by Christ's Spirit to the heavenly Tabernacle and sprinkled on the mercy seat

(Lev. 16:14–15; Heb.9:13–14).This had to occur before the soldier's spear inflicted the postmortal injury, causing the residual blood and water to flow freely from his side onto the ground to the amazement of the Apostle (Jn. 19:34–35)! Previous to the time of death from such a fatal haemorrhage, the skin capillaries would have contracted down to prevent a fall in blood pressure, causing a blanching of the victim's skin. When death ensues, the same skin blood vessels dilate, causing a crimson blushing of the skin to gradually spread over the body (postmortem lividity).

4. Christ's Death

On the day before his death, Jesus attended a last supper with his disciples. At this communion he grasped the opportunity to explain the predestined pattern of his atoning sacrifice, in which he was to fulfil the two vital roles, in suffering as a sin-bearing Saviour and dying as a Redeemer.

Firstly, the breaking of the bread at the beginning of the remembrance meal was to signify the breaking of his body; this was to declare his vicarious inheritance of the sins of this world, the initial part-payment of the ransom price of redemption.

Secondly, the wine he offered at the end of the Passover signified the shedding of his precious blood, thus fulfilling the requirement of the Law expressed in the language of Christ's altar.

Isaac Watts immortalised a graphic visual observation on the two vital stages of Christ's death in his great hymn concerning the Crucifixion, entitled,

'When I survey the wondrous cross on which the Prince of Glory died, –'

In this hymn, a theological genius described the same two sacrificial roles in subsequent verses.

Stage one: Verse 3. Christ's passion.
'See from his head, his hands, his feet, sorrow and love flow mingled down:
did e'er such love and sorrow meet, or thorns compose so rich a crown.'

Stage two: Verse 4. Christ's death,
followed by a believer's response.

'The dying crimson, like a robe, spreads o'er his body on the tree.
Then am I dead to all the globe, and all the globe is dead to me.'

The significance of these two theological statements must be viewed in the light of a conceivable personal experience; for in the 17th century, the Rev. Isaac Watts served as a Congregational Minister in the port of Southampton, when it was not unusual for young adults to die from hidden, but none the less torrential and fatal blood loss!

Such a fatal haemorrhage might be caused either accidentally or from a spontaneous internal haemorrhage! In that era, a 'man of the cloth' could well be called to pray for a young man who had fallen from a great height in the shipyards and suffered a massive internal bleeding from a ruptured spleen, or to a young woman haemorrhaging from an ectopic pregnancy!

On each occasion, he would have witnessed the initial blanching of the victim's skin, imminently followed by the spread of a crimson discolouration over the whole body heralding impending death. At first, there would be a crimson flush of the feet, spreading up the legs to the lower part of the trunk. This would be quickly followed by a similar crimson flushing of the hands, spreading up the arms to involve the head and chest. So the whole surface area of the body, including the face, changed from an initial pallor to a bright crimson colour. These colour changes create a startling appearance to anyone, with the possible exclusion of most professional observers!

Therefore, it is likely that Isaac Watts had gained such personal experience, which made him capable of describing the vivid death of his Saviour from the cryptic shedding of his blood upon the cross of Golgotha! It was no wonder that the centurion and those with him were terrified with such vivid appearances apparent at the death of the Son of God (Mt. 27:54; Mk. 15:39; Lk. 23:47–48). Fortunately, in this country such cases of catastrophic death have been radically reduced by modern medical emergency services, which means that fewer people have this personal experience enabling them to appreciate the significance of Isaac Watts' observations. This lack of experience has led many publishers to exclude the crucial verse four from this famous hymn!

When surveying Christ's wondrous cross, sacrifice and death, it behoves every believer to recognise the personal debt owed to our heavenly Father for the indescribable gift of giving himself in the person of his only Son for our salvation (Jn. 3:16; 2 Cor. 9:15). Such an act of homage should be part of one's daily confession of the gospel of Christ.

A realistic recognition of the surpassing grace of our heavenly Father is far better rendered at Christ's altar, the cross of Golgotha. It is not being suggested that every believer should visit the Holy Sepulchre in Jerusalem, although nobody should be dissuaded from such an awesome and inspiring pilgrimage. It is a harrowing experience, climbing the steep steps towards the summit of the execution rock. The haunting words of Elizabeth Clephane's hymn kept repeating in one's mind,

'Upon the cross of Jesus, mine eyes at times can see,
The very dying form of one, who suffered there for me.
And from my smitten heart, with tears, two wonders I confess,
The wonder of his glorious love and my own worthlessness.'

The same awesome experience is gained by visiting Christ's cross in the paradisiacal kingdom of heaven in prayerful worship. This throne of grace is approachable to every believer through God's great plan of redemption (Ps. 143:8 K.J.V; 2 Cor. 12:3–4; Heb. 4:16). It is his divine reward, for the recognition of our Saviour's atoning sacrifice (Heb. 2:10)! The experience provides one with the opportunity to truly plead for his forgiving grace. In response, we receive the supreme privilege of being led by the Holy Spirit through the veil of Christ's body (his righteousness) into the heavenly sanctuary. This is the divine approach into the most holy presence of the heavenly Father, which is available to all believers!

5. The Blood of Christ

Under the Mosaic-Levitical covenants, the sanctified High Priest collected and carried the sacrificial blood in clean bronze bowls. This was to keep it unsoiled and prevent it from clotting, allowing the sacrifice to be sprinkled on the altar and also onto various parts of the sanctuary, including the atonement cover upon the mercy seat (Lev. 15:15–16). Any residual blood was poured out at the foot of the altar and covered with soil.

If the major portion of the crucified Lord's blood had been shed cryptically into his abdomen or belly (as the cause of his death, previously described) it would have remained pure and uncongealed. This would have provided Christ's Spirit the opportunity to collect and convey his blood to the heavenly Sanctuary, to obtain posthumous atonement and eternal redemption from the sins of this world vicariously imputed upon him (Heb. 9:11–15 *see* page 123). Such a metaphysical or supernatural transfer had to take place within the first three hours after his death, before the soldier pierced his side with a spear. For if this divine conveyance had not occurred, the postmortem wound would otherwise have caused all of Christ's sacrificial blood, mingled with water, to flow onto the foot of his cross or altar and become contaminated and unfit for atonement (Jn. 19:34–37; Heb. 13:10)!

In this way, Christ's atoning sacrifice fulfilled the exact regulations for the eternal plan of divine atonement. These were included in the copies, which were handed down to Moses to convey God's first Covenant to the Israelites. Christ's blood paid the ransom price for the redemption of all who believe in him, cleansing our consciences (Heb. 9:14). So it could be said,

"To God's elect – who have been chosen according to the foreknowledge of God the Father, through the sanctifying work of the Spirit, for obedience to Jesus Christ and the sprinkling by his blood."

(1 Pe. 1:1–2)

6. Christ our Great High Priest

The LORD said to my Lord,
"Sit at my right hand,
until I make your enemies
a footstool for your feet."
The LORD has sworn,
and will not change his mind,
"You are a priest for ever
in the order of Melchizedek."

(*Ps. 110:1 and 4*)

Even before Christ's birth, the Jews believed this psalm of David prophesied the advent of their Anointed One, the promised King-Priest. For it contained the two Oracles revealing God's will, (*see* reference under 'the Anointed One', page 67).

Jesus quoted the first Oracle (verse one) when he was teaching in the temple courts. They were recorded later in the first three Gospels (Mt. 22:43–45, Mk. 12:36–37 and Lk. 20:42–44). Peter also quoted them when he was preaching about the risen Lord Jesus Christ (Acts 2:29–36), whom he had previously declared to be the Messiah, Son of the living God (Mt. 16:16; Mk. 8:27–29 and Lk. 9:18–20). Therefore in retrospect, this prophecy was not referring to the promised advent of the Anointed One, but to the coronation of the risen Lord Jesus Christ!

The second Oracle (verse four) announced this great High Priest would rule forever under the ancient order of Melchizedek. This meant a change of priesthood from the old Levitical order that had failed to fulfil the promises of the Covenant LORD.

Under the New Covenant, the disciples accepted Jesus to be their Saviour (Lk. 1:47, 2:11, Jn. 4:42) bringing salvation to those who loved and believed in him (Lk. 1:69, 1:71 and 77, 2:30, 3:6, 19:9). Originally, Jesus taught his disciples the Lord's Prayer (Lk. 11:1–4), by which he instructed them to follow his example and pray directly to the heavenly Father. Later he told them that when he had left this world, he would send the Holy Spirit to help guide them in all truth. Then they should no longer ask of him anything, but were to ask the Father in his name (Jn. 16:15, 23–24)! Yet they never claimed him to be their High Priest or advocate, while he was with them in this world!

On the night of his betrayal, Jesus prayed for all those whom his Father had given him that he might give them eternal life. This not only included his disciples, but also for all those who would eventually believe in him and help spread the Gospel to others. This prayer is often referred to as the Lord's High Priestly Prayer (Jn. 17:1–26) as it reveals the true depth of Christ's devotion for all those the Father has given him!

After the resurrection, apart from John's referral to Jesus Christ being our advocate with the heavenly Father (1 Jn. 2:1), it was left to Paul to ascribe to his Lord the fulfilment of three of the most important High-Priestly duties. These included,

1. Christ being the provider of the sacrifice for atonement, through faith and righteousness (Ro. 3:24–28)
2. Christ Jesus sitting at the right hand of the Father, interceding for us (Ro. 8:34)
3. Christ reconciling us to God (2 Cor. 5:18–19)

Later, in his letters to the Colossian Church (Col. 1:15–20), the Apostle was led to record his belief on the risen Lord, as concerning,

'The Supremacy of Christ, Son of God.'

"He is the image of the invisible God, the first born over all creation.
For by him all things were created, things in heaven and on earth,
visible and invisible, whether thrones or powers or rulers or authorities:
all things were created by him and for him.
He is before all things, and in him all things hold together.
And he is the head of the body, the church.
He is the beginning and the firstborn from among the dead.
So that in everything he might have supremacy.
For God was pleased to have all his fullness dwell in him.
And through him to reconcile to himself all things, whether things on earth or things
in heaven, by making peace through his blood, shed on the cross."

This Pauline theology was developed later in the Epistle to the Hebrews, in which Jesus is described as our High Priest, forever, after the order of Melchizedek (Heb.4:14–16, 5:1–10)!

7. Conclusions

In this chapter evidence is provided to verify God's fulfilment of his divine Messianic promises previously revealed by the Old Testament prophets, in reference to Christ's atoning sacrifice and death. Added to which the significance of his shed blood has proved beyond all doubt that Christ not only fulfilled, but also continues to fulfil the duties of our Great High Priest. This evidence had been divinely revealed from the very beginning of creation, being a fundamental example of the unfolding of God's great plan of redemption for his chosen people (Jn.3:16).

The greatest promise of the New and Eternal covenant is the gift of eternal life, to be spent in the paradisiacal kingdom of heaven. It is given to all who love, trust and obey the Son. It is the hidden treasure, or fine pearl, found in the hearts of all believers (Mt.13:44–45). Jesus Christ is the 'tree of life' bridging the gulf or linking believers in this world to his Father's kingdom in heaven!

If further evidence be needed to prove that Jesus of Nazareth was the only true Son of God, the Anointed One, then his ancestry, birth and the fulfilment of his ministry in the Year of the LORD'S favour are found hidden in the Old Testament, as previously revealed. The same can be said concerning his death. His ancestry recorded by Matthew has been referred to in the introductory part of the last chapter. Added to this is a more detailed bloodline, which includes the ancestry of his mother Mary. It traces the genealogy of Jesus back in reverse order to Adam, who was described as a son of God. This was fully recorded by Luke, the Greek scholar and physician, and friend of Paul (Lk. 3:23–37).

Therefore, by the time their Anointed One was born, the Hebrews had been provided with more than sufficient divine evidence needed for them to celebrate the advent of their promised Saviour and Redeemer. God the Father heralded the birth of his Son through his angels. Gabriel was sent first to a priest named Zechariah, a descendant of Aaron who served in the temple. He was told that his wife would give birth to a son and he was to give him the name John (Lk. 1:11–17). He would be born with the spirit and power of Elijah, who according to Hebraic tradition would appear before the coming of the Messiah (Mal. 4:5–6).

Later, Gabriel visited a virgin called Mary and announced to her that she would become the mother of a son and he was to be given the name Jesus. At the same time, it was prophesied,

"He will be great and will be called the Son of the Most High.
The Lord God will give him the throne of his father David,
and he will reign over the house of Jacob forever; his kingdom will never end."
(Lk. 1:32–33)

Therefore this advent fulfilled all the prophecies included in the Scroll of the Law given to Moses, which was sacrosanct according to Hebraic tradition! Still later, when Jesus was presented by his parents at the Temple, for the purification rites required by the Law of Moses, there was a righteous and devote Hebrew named Simeon who was waiting for the consolation and salvation of Israel (Isa. 40:1–2; 52:9–10). He took the child, Jesus, in his arms and prophesied what had been revealed to him by the Holy Spirit,

"For my eyes have seen your salvation,
which you have prepared in the sight of all people,
a light for revelation to the Gentiles,
and for glory to your people Israel."
(Lk. 2:30–33)

At the same time, there was also a prophet, Anna, who never left the temple;

"She gave thanks to God and spoke about the child
to all who were looking forward to the redemption of Jerusalem."
(Lk. 2:38)

Yet, the Apostle John recorded later,

"He was in the world, and the world was made by him and the world knew him not –
He came unto his own and his own received him not –"
(Jn. 1:30-31. K.J.V.)

At the height of his ministry, John the Baptist sent two of his disciples to ask Jesus if he were the one who was to come.

Jesus' reply was as previously proclaimed (Lk. 4:18–19, *see* page 89).

"Go back and report to John what you have seen and heard,
the blind receive sight, the lame walk, those who have leprosy are cured,
the deaf hear, the dead are raised, and the good news is proclaimed to the poor!"
(Lk. 7:22–23)

This fulfilled the prophecies of Isaiah, concerning the Messiah (Isa. 29:18–19; 35:5–6; 61:1–2).

Finally,

'The early Christian church had to overcome the charms of the old Levitical Covenant.
Its venerable ancientness had a powerful influence destined for perpetual endurance.'
(John Brown)

It not only dissuaded the Jews from accepting Christianity, but also influenced those who became Christian converts to hold fast to some of its orthodox ceremonial practices e.g. circumcision. Paul's messages to the early Christian converts were aimed at correcting any excessive and ignorant veneration of the nature and design of the Mosaic institutions. In his letter to the Roman Church, he warned the Jews of the danger of relying on the Mosaic Law and their bragging over their relationship to God (Ro. 2:1–24). Their faith in the *Sepher Torah* was incomparable to the salvation gained through Christ, reconciling them through his atoning sacrifice (Col. 1:15–23).

Later, Paul appealed to the Church in Corinth,

"We implore you on Christ's behalf: Be reconciled to God.
God made him who had no sin to be sin for us,
So that in him we might become the righteousness of God."
(2 Cor. 5:20–21)

Martin Luther described this divine act of imputation in the following words,

'Lord Jesus you are my righteousness.
I am your sin.
You took on you, what was mine,
Yet set on me what was yours.
You became what you were not, that I might become what I was not!'

CHAPTER 6

NEW TESTAMENT CONFIRMATION
as recorded in The Epistle of Paul to the Hebrews
(K.J.V.)

1. Introduction

On the Day of Pentecost, fifty days after the crucifixion of Jesus of Nazareth and Passover, the risen Lord gathered his disciples together to receive the Holy Spirit and inaugurate the first Hebrew-Christian Church. Over the early years, as the membership grew throughout Asia Minor, it came to include four highly intelligent, intellectual, Jewish Christians. These were Paul, Luke, Barnabas and Apollos, each in turn having been held to be the unidentified author of a collection of letters or possibly essays that were written to the Hebrew members of the original Church in Jerusalem. Although the style and the scholarly diction have long been considered not to be Pauline in character, the depths of the writer's power of persuasion were instinctively those of the Apostle. He might well have dictated the content to the scholastic Barnabas, Apollos, or even Luke the physician, as their main qualifications for authorship included a familiarity with Paul's doctrinal teaching. All four were knowledgeable concerning the content of the pre-Christian Greek translation of the Old Testament Scripture, later called the Septuagint or its Latin abbreviation LXX, which was frequently referred to throughout the letters. It eventually became the new 'Torah' or Bible that was used to evangelise the Jews and Gentile members of the early Christian Church!

The Septuagint is considered by many to be another fundamental example of the unfolding plan of God's good grace towards mankind, being a translation of the *Sepher Torah* and the remaining books of the Old Testament from Hebrew into Greek by seventy Jewish scholars. The LXX contained the Scroll of the Law of God that had been entrusted to the Hebrew race, but they dishonoured its divine authority by failing to live up to the holy commands (Gal. 3:10–11). It had been selfishly treasured and coveted as their privileged possession, for they had little respect towards other races; traditionally the orthodox Jew considered a slave to be 'a breathing tool' and the Gentiles were no more valuable than dogs in their sight. With few exceptions, there had been no previous attempts to evangelise the word of God during the thousand or more years of their stewardship. Therefore the translation of the Hebrew Script into Greek made in the third century B.C. (250 years before the Christian era) meant that it could be heard and understood by the emigrant Jews outside the Holy Land who no longer spoke their Hebrew tongue and also by many Gentile converts to the faith.

It was the first step towards future translations of both Old and New Testaments into Vulgar Latin by Jerome in 1454 A.D. (The Vulgate Bible) and during the next century into German (Luther) French (Calvin) and English (Wycliffe, Tyndale and Coverdale). These translations initiated and fulfilled the last prophecy of Jesus to his disciples, before his ascension into heaven:

"And you will be my witnesses in Jerusalem, and in all Judea and Samaria, and to the ends of the earth."

(Ac. 1:8)

Finally, it is believed that Paul spent the last two years of his life in solitary confinement (66–67 A.D.) chained to a post in a Roman prison, with Luke and probably Onesiphorus attending to his welfare. During this time, it is said that he wrote or dictated his second and last letter to Timothy. Traditionally, it is also believed that for the last nine months of their lives both Paul and Simon Peter were held possibly together in the same Roman prison up until their deaths on the same day (29th June 67 A.D.) Peter was crucified and Paul executed (Pollock).

As it is accepted that the Epistle to the Hebrews was written before 70 A.D., Paul could well have been the author, having written or dictated the contents in which he speaks of himself being in bonds (Heb. 10:34. K.J.V.). Therefore, up to the time of the Reformation, it was generally believed that Paul was the undisputed author.

In 1534, William Tyndale published his New Testament, containing 'The Epistle of St. Paul unto the Hebrews', translated from the earliest Hebrew and Greek texts. In the Prolegomena, it is clear that he was aware of the disputation over its authorship, but refused to comment other than to state that the epistle was godly and of great learning. In his translation, Tyndale not only entitled the Epistle to be that of St. Paul to the Hebrews, but also elevated the book above the epistles of Peter and John to the penultimate position in relation to the Revelation of St. John the Divine. Only two short letters from James and Judas, who were brothers of Jesus, separated the two books! Subsequently, Tyndale's translations were included in Coverdale's Bible and eventually handed down to the King James Bible, in which Paul's authorship of the epistle is still retained in modern day Authorised versions. Added to this belief, John Brown's Exposition of Hebrews leaves little scope for doubt about the true author being none other than the Apostle to the Gentiles (Ro. 11:13)!

It is also believed that the fundamental doctrines included in the letters were written for the large number of Jews converted to Christianity, including orthodox Hebrew priests who were wavering because of their rigid upbringings (Ac. 6:7 N.I.V. *see* fn.). The aim was to persuade them to become obedient to the principles of their new faith in the Lord Jesus Christ, the Messiah!

Content

This book contains invaluable and authentic information, which highlights the fundamental doctrines of Old Testament Scripture and compares them to the supremacy and sufficiency of the new Christian faith, as previously recorded in the New Testament teachings. It summarises and compares the superiority of Jesus, the author and prophet of the New Eternal Covenant, to Moses who was the author and prophet of the Old Covenant.

The content provides some staggering information concerning the Old Covenant, which proved Moses to be a faithful servant in all God's house, bearing witness to that spoken by God concerning the future (Heb. 3:5). Having quoted the prophecy of Jeremiah concerning the declaration of the future New Covenant, the writer declares the failure of the Old Covenant to be entirely due to the unfaithfulness of the Israelites. Also,

"By calling this covenant, 'new,' he (God) has made the first one obsolete; and what is obsolete and outdated will soon disappear."

(Heb. 8:13)

Hebrews is divided into two parts, the first being doctrinal and the second practical; the former includes the first nine chapters and the first eighteen verses of the tenth chapter, whereas the latter is the remainder of the tenth and the eleventh chapter. It is not intended to provide a detailed view of all the content, but only to highlight any new evidence confirming our previous findings concerning the Eternal Covenant from the Gospels and Epistles of the New Testament.

The first two chapters of Hebrews compare the superiority of the personality and preaching of Jesus Christ, the Son of God, to Moses and the angels who were highly rated in Hebrew faith. The third chapter highlights the High-Priesthood of Jesus Christ, approved of by his divine appointments and his superiority to the previous priesthoods under the old Levitical Covenant. The content is very similar to that described in the Gospels and other Epistles, as previously outlined. There is little addition, as both revelations are mainly factual, but there is far greater clarification.

2. The Book of 'HEBREWS'

In the first four verses of this book, God speaks to mankind by his Son, through the Holy Spirit. Many theologians believe that Paul was entrusted to write these gracious words in 67 A.D., possibly during his second and final Roman imprisonment.

Although it is thought that he was chained to a post during his final incarceration, this would not have prevented him from dictating a final letter to the Hebrew converts in the early Christian church. It has a most wonderful and powerful prologue, entitled,

'The Superiority of Christ, Son of God.'
"In the past God spoke to our forefathers through the prophets
at many times and in various ways,
but in these last days, he has spoken to us by his Son,
whom he appointed heir of all things, and
through whom he made the universe.
The Son is the radiance of God's glory and the exact representation of his being,
Sustaining all things by the power of his word.
After he had provided purification for sins,
he sat down at the right hand of the Majesty in heaven.
So he became as much superior to the angels
as the name he has inherited is superior to theirs."

The content is comparable to a similar text when God spoke to mankind concerning his Son through the Holy Spirit, on a previous occasion. Then the divine words were entrusted to Paul in 60 A.D., who recorded them in his letter to Christians in the Colossian Church, during his first Roman imprisonment. They were entitled, **'The Supremacy of Christ, Son of God.'** and are to be found on Page 102.

Each text holds the divine mysteries of Jesus Christ, the

only Son of God and when brought together they express his glory, as previously recorded by the Apostle John in the prologue of his gospel:

"The glory of the One and Only, who came from the Father, full of grace and truth."

N.B. whereas '**The Superiority of Christ, Son of God**' is printed in bold Roman letters, '***The Supremacy of Christ, Son of God.***' is printed in bold italics, but only on this occasion to differentiate it from the former text.

The combined texts are as follows,

'In the past God spoke to our forefathers through the prophets
at many times and in various ways,
but in these last days, he has spoken to us by his Son.
The Son is the radiance of God's glory and the exact representation of his being.
He is the image of the invisible God, the first born of all creation.
Through whom God made the universe,
for by him all things were created, things in heaven and on earth.
Therefore he is heir of all things, sustaining them by the power of his word.
After he had provided purification for sins,
making peace through his blood upon the cross,
he sat down at the right hand of the Majesty in heaven.
He is the beginning and the firstborn from among the dead.
So he became superior to the angels,

As the name he inherited is superior to theirs.
So in everything he might have supremacy.
For God was pleased to have all his fullness dwell in him.
And through him to reconcile to himself all things,
whether things on earth or in heaven.

The two texts when read together express the fundamental doctrines of God's unfolding plan of salvation, being not only congruous, but also complementary to one another. Can there be any doubt that the risen Lord chose anyone other than the same servant, to herald his Father's proclamations on each occasion?

3. The Primacy of Jesus Christ

The underlying purpose of these letters was to persuade the early Christian Hebrews to give up their belief and practice of the traditional Hebrew rites they had observed before their conversion. To fulfil this one desire, the Apostle had to spend some time comparing Jesus Christ's achievements, as High Priest of the New Covenant, to those of Aaron and his descendants who were High Priests of the Old Covenant. In addition he set out to compare the Lord Jesus to Moses, who was and still remains legendary in the sight of the Israelite and Hebrew race. Finally, he compares the Lord Jesus to the angels, whom the Jews held in high esteem, as messengers from God holding a powerful influence over their day-to-day observance of the Levitical law.

4. Jesus our High Priest

The High Priests of the Old Covenant,

'were taken from among men and ordained for men
in the things pertaining to God,
to offer gifts and sacrifices for sins, in order to
bring men into the favourable presence of God –
to be reckoned and treated by God as his people.'
(John Brown)

Whereas Jesus Christ as Prophet and High Priest of the New Covenant offers free access to God's most holy presence. He not only became the High Priest, but also had to provide the sacrificial atonement, because the heavenly Father demanded a perfect and sinless sacrifice to pacify the divine wrath against the corruption of his creation. Therefore Christ elected to suffer and die to provide pardon for our sins, foreknowing that he was the only perfect and acceptable Lamb of God!

Our great High Priest, the risen Lord, is a priest forever of the order of Melchizedek. He serves continually in the sanctuary of the heavenly Tabernacle, set up by God before the beginning of creation (Heb. 8:1). Since Jesus had a heavenly Father and was born of a woman, he was compared to King Melchizedek, who according to Hebraic tradition was without trace of a human father or mother and without genealogy. This sets both of them apart from the Aaronical and Levitical priesthoods, whose selection was based on human heredity! Also, these priests had to retire when fifty years old; but King Melchizedek resembled the Son of God in remaining a priest forever, without the beginning of days or end of life, as his birth and death were never recorded.

It should be noted, however, this was simply a resemblance between them, as Melchizedek was only a man. There is no real evidence to suggest that he was a manifestation, or a prefiguration (a theophany) of Jesus Christ, by sharing in an eternal priesthood (Heb. 7:1–19). Yet these two differences drew a line between the order of Aaronical succession of High Priests under the Old Covenant and the order under the new economy! In retrospect, King Melchizedek must have been an extraordinary and wonderful person, to be created to inaugurate and establish a High Priesthood that had been destined to become the divine order chosen for the only Son of God! Yet it is conceivable that he was not only the revered ancestor of Abram and King David, but also of Jesus of Nazareth, his Saviour and Redeemer.

5. Jesus Compared to Moses

Under the New Covenant, the author of Hebrews claimed Jesus to be even greater than Moses, as our Apostle and High Priest and as the Son over God's house. Although Jesus strikingly resembled Moses, he more certainly excelled him as a legislator of divine law.

Moses was an Apostle of God (*saliah*) having been given the two stone tablets of the Testimony (Ex. 31:18) and was subsequently authorised to expound the established Law of the Old Testament. In comparison, Jesus Christ is a Prophet and High Priest of the New Covenant providing free access to God's most holy presence through the Holy Spirit (Eph. 2:18). He has also suffered, himself, to gain pardon for our sins; for in the words of the Apostle,

> **"In him we have redemption through his blood,**
> **the forgiveness of sins,**
> **in accordance with the riches of God's grace**
> **that he lavished on us."**
>
> **(Eph. 1:7)**

Moses was shepherding Jethro's sheep when first called by the hand of God to become the fully prepared saviour of the enslaved Israelites in Egypt. After leading that great escape, he became the ruler over the Israelite tribe, God's chosen people. He was called to the summit of Sinai, the mountain of the LORD, to receive the Covenant containing the 'former regulations of divine worship' and government that were superior to anything human wisdom could ever conceive or devise. For forty years in the Sinai desert, Moses ruled wisely over the affairs of the Israelites, regardless of their misbelief and rebellion in the sight of God. Above all that, he built a temporary house for God to dwell and instructed the people in the LORD's commands on how to worship (Ex. 34:34).God's earthly tabernacle was also a sanctuary for his most holy presence, as in the paradisiacal kingdom of heaven (Heb. 8:5).

In comparison, Jesus Christ serves as our High Priest in the eternal sanctuary,

"The true Tabernacle set up by the Lord, not by man"

(Heb. 8:1–2)

Therefore, Moses ranked highly in Hebraic leadership up to the time of the early Christian Church; its doubting members were now called upon to consider his successor,

"The Apostle and High Priest of our profession, Jesus Christ."

(Heb. 3:1. K.J.V.)

Finally, it must be remembered that Jesus Christ revealed not only his glory, but also his superiority on the Mount of Transfiguration, when Moses and Elijah were summoned to attend and prepare him for his final departure (Mt. 17:1–6; Mk. 9:2–13; Lk. 9:28–36).

6. Jesus Compared to the Angels

To enforce the Supremacy of Jesus Christ and the New Covenant it was also necessary to draw a comparison to the angels, as well as to Moses, because God created the angels ever before mankind. The Jews feared the presence of the angels, believing them to be the messengers (*malak* in Hebrew and *angelos* in Greek) of the LORD. Although they accepted the Spirit of heaven to be the power of the Most High God, as revealed by his awesome breath (*ruach)* and in the wisdom expressed by his word (*dabar*), they believed the inspired infallible statements concerning the will of God were revealed to the prophets by the angels in the forms of dreams and visions (Heb. 1:14). The Jews also trusted implicitly the promise received from God and expressed by the psalmist,

"For he shall give his angels charge over thee, to keep thee in all thy ways.
They shall bear thee up in their hands, lest thou dash thy foot against a stone."

(Ps. 91:11-12. K.J.V.)

(Jesus quoted these words, when the devil tempted him in the desert – Mt. 4:5–6)

Therefore the angels were held in the position of highest authority in Hebraic tradition, as with "the angel of the Lord" (Ps. 34:7, 148:2). Even the seraphs were awesome when the sound of their voices shook the temple and filled it with smoke (Isa. 6:2–4)! According to Talmudic legend there were four archangels who stood around the throne of God. They included Michael, Gabriel, Uriel and Raphael. Michael appeared to Daniel in a vision, as being the chief prince who protects the children of God (Dan. 10:9; 12:1) He was named later for his fight with his angels against the dragon in heaven (Rev. 12:7–9).

Finally, it must not be forgotten that Lucifer was once described as, 'the morning star, son of the dawn'. He was considered to be the most beautiful and powerful member of the celestial creation. This was before he rebelled, to be cast out of heaven and cut down to earth (Isa. 14:12–15; Lk. 10:18) becoming the Old Testament adversary called '*Satan*' (Hebrew). Jesus and his followers were fully aware of the devil's awesome powers (Mt. 4:1–11; Lk. 4:2; Jn. 6:70; Eph. 4:27).

In the New Testament there was an early flourish of angelic activity, appearing as messengers from God, there being many references to their existence throughout the Gospels! Gabriel's visit to Zechariah has already been noted, bringing the good news concerning the birth of a son, John the Baptist. When his authority was questioned, he announced,

"I am Gabriel, I stand in the presence of God."
(Lk. 1:19)

God sent Gabriel to Nazareth to visit Mary and announce the good news concerning the birth of Jesus (Lk. 1:31). Later an angel of the Lord appeared to Joseph (Mt. 1:20–21) and to the shepherds heralding the good news that a Saviour, the Messiah, had been born in Bethlehem (Lk. 2: 8–12).

Then in the desert when Satan tempted Jesus, the angels came and attended him (Mt. 4:1–11). After the crucifixion, when the two women visited Jesus' tomb on the first day, an angel of the Lord came down from heaven and rolled back the stone to reveal he had risen (Mt. 28:2–7). But angelic appearances diminished after the resurrection. Following the inauguration of the Christian Church, their influence became subservient to the power of the Holy Spirit in revealing God's will. Their biblical recordings faded, apart from the time of Peter's imprisonment when an angel was sent to free and help him to escape (Ac. 12:7).

Therefore the New Testament doctrine of the risen Lord Jesus Christ places him in superiority far above all other divine powers in heaven and upon this earth (Col. 1:15–20). The Apostle clarified the 'status quo' by warning the orthodox Jews that their worship of God through angels was a false teaching and in his letter to the Hebrews he stressed the superiority of Christ as the perfect mediator with the heavenly Father (Heb. 1:4–13).

7. Final Comparison

The last chapters of the doctrinal first part of the book of Hebrews contain an ultimate comparison between the Old and New Covenants, each one being made by God for his chosen peoples. The author finally stresses the superiority of Christian worship over and above the former Mosaic regulations for the Israelites and Hebrews.

In the first section of the ninth chapter, the regulations for worship in the Mosaic tabernacle are followed by a summarised description of its plan and content, imposing a three-step pattern of approach in their worship of the Covenant LORD. It is then pointedly observed that,

"The Holy Spirit was showing by this that the way into the Most Holy Place had not yet been disclosed as long as the first tabernacle was still standing."

(Heb. 9:8)

The failure of the Mosaic pattern of worship was an awesome reminder to the early Christian Jews, persuading them that the gifts and sacrifices they had previously been taught to offer were no longer acceptable and failed to clear their consciences of sin.

In comparison, the second section of the chapter reveals that the risen Lord fulfilled his High Priestly duties to perfection, by entering and passing through the heavenly Tabernacle, greater and more perfectly constructed by God.

"He did not enter by means of the blood of goats and calves,
but he entered the Most Holy Place once for all by his own blood,
thus obtaining eternal redemption"

(Heb. 9:12)

His own blood redeemed the Saviour of our sins that were imputed upon him on the cross. He was then enabled to purchase righteousness for those who believe in his atoning sacrifice.

"How much more then will the blood of Christ, who through the eternal Spirit offered himself unblemished to God, cleanse our consciences from acts that lead to death, so that we may serve the living God."

(Heb. 9:14)

Therefore Christ became the mediator of the New Covenant between his heavenly Father and those called to receive the promised eternal inheritance,

"Now that he had died as a ransom to set them free from the sins committed under the Old Covenant."

(Heb. 9:15)

Christ's death was essential for him to be able to provide the blood required to seal the New Covenant, as was the sacrificial lifeblood of animals required to seal the Old Covenant,

"for without the shedding of blood, there is no forgiveness."

(Heb. 9:22. *see* p.98)

Finally, in the tenth chapter, the Apostle outlined the sufficiency of Christ's sacrifice. He points out to the Jewish converts the weakness of the laws and commands of Moses, being only a shadow or reflection of the things to come. God's instruction to Moses concerning sacrificial worship was given simply to remind his people of their sins, the proof being declared in David's psalm (40:6–8):

"With burnt offerings and sin offerings you were not pleased.
Then I said, 'Here am I – it is written about me in the scroll –
I have come to do your will, my God."
(Heb. 10:6–7)

To this the Apostle adds,

"And by that will,
we have been made holy through the sacrifice of the body of Christ once for all."
(Heb. 10:10)

Following the completion of Christ's atoning sacrifice, the heavenly Father called the Son into his very presence in the Heaven of Heavens. He was invited to sit at God's right hand and continue to make supplications for all who believe in him. The Holy Spirit testifies that God has sworn,

"Their sins and lawless acts, I will remember no more."
(Heb. 10:17)

This meant that worldly sacrifices were no longer required for their forgiveness and Hebrew converts to Christianity should not doubt the sufficiency of Christ's sacrifice. They should also recognise his elevation to the supreme position of great High Priest to the eternal house of God in heavenly places.

As a forerunner, God provides every believer with the confidence to follow his Holy Spirit through the curtain or veil of Christ's body. His sacrifice opened up a new and living way into the Most Holy Place of the paradisiacal Tabernacle; so every believer might draw near to the most holy presence of the heavenly Father, through the mediation of his Son.

8. Final Encouragement

The second part of this book written to the Hebrews contains further instructions for the wavering new converts, combined with sound practical advice concerning their new Christian faith. The Apostle does not withhold the reality of the situation, for the Law of God prevails in the new divine plan of faith and must be obeyed. But the return of the risen Lord Jesus, the Second Advent, brings the promise of immortal life and happiness to every believer. This promise was heralded previously in the Gospels.

"God having provided some better thing for us –"
(Heb. 11:40. K.J.V.)

N.B. This part of the apostolic message contains two urgent appeals, followed by two commands, each being summarised in the following texts from the tenth chapter,

First Appeal

"Therefore, brothers and sisters, since we have
confidence to enter the Most Holy Place
by the blood of Jesus, by a new and living way
opened for us
through the curtain that is, his body, – "
(Heb. 10:19-20)

This most difficult passage of Scripture has in the past caused much debate and controversy centred on the identity and locality of the Most Holy Place.

Some believe that the Most Holy Place refers to the Heaven of Heavens, described as the seventh heaven, where God the Father lives alone. John Brown made the point that the risen Lord entered and passed through the heavenly Tabernacle, sprinkling his sacrificial blood to cleanse the content, before entering bodily into the Holy of Holies. He carried his body, being his glorified human nature, into the very presence of God consecrating a new and living way for believers to follow in confidence!

Yet this view is incongruous with that recorded in the fourth Gospel, for the Apostle John clearly states in his Prologue,

"No one has ever seen God (the heavenly Father), but God the One and Only (the Son), who is at the Father's side, has made him known."

(Jn. 1:18)

So there is little doubt that in this first appeal the Apostle is repeating his previous reference to the entry into the inner sanctuary behind the curtain (Heb. 8:2; *see* N.I.V.fn.). Our forerunner, Jesus Christ, entered there on our behalf as our High Priest of the order of Melchizedek (Heb. 6:19–20). Therefore, our Saviour and Redeemer opened up a new and living way through the curtain between the Holy and the Most Holy Places, for those who believe in him to follow in his steps! This sanctuary of the heavenly Tabernacle is the only approachable place where the most holy presence of our infinite and omnipresent heavenly Father exists.

At the time of Christ's death on the cross, the veil or curtain separating the Holy Place from the Most Holy Place was rent in two (Lk. 23:45) allowing a conditional access to the inner sanctuary for all believers in daily worship during their lives in this world! Therefore, we may approach the very presence of the heavenly Father within the Tabernacle of the paradisiacal kingdom of heaven, as did the psalmist of old (Ps. 18:6; 100:4), but only when covered by Christ's righteousness (the garments of his salvation) and through his mediation!

Second Appeal

"Since we have a great priest over the house of God, let us draw near to God with a sincere heart in full assurance of faith, having our hearts sprinkled to cleanse us from a guilty conscience and having our bodies washed with pure water.- "

(Heb. 10:21)

The book of Leviticus is a manual of the regulations given to Moses, concerning the service of worship in the tabernacle set up by God. It relates that the Israelites were not allowed to draw near to God's most holy presence, except through the mediation of their High Priest. This regulation was highlighted on Atonement Day, the only day in the year when the High Priest was allowed entry into the Most Holy Place to plead in the presence of the Covenant LORD for his people.

Yet we have a personal access to our heavenly Father's most holy presence through our infinitely superior High

Priest at all times during our lives (Isa. 58:9). This spiritual approach is facilitated through the 'ordinances of divine worship' practised in the heavenly Tabernacle. It was laid down before creation and was reflected in the copies of instructions given to Moses on the mountain, for worship in the earthly tabernacle. As we have a great High Priest over the house of God, in the Tabernacle of the paradisiacal kingdom of heaven, our worship and prayers are acceptable through the mediation of our risen Lord. So let us praise God with this assurance, the foundation of our authority being a personal faith in Jesus Christ. But we must not fail to recognise two vital conditions in the second half of the text, which provide the confidence to draw near to a holy God.

The first condition is having, 'our hearts sprinkled, to cleanse us from a guilty conscience'. This refers to Christ's atoning sacrifice; as Moses sprinkled the people with the blood of the Old Covenant, Christ sprinkles every believer with his blood of the New Covenant.

The second condition is having our bodies washed with pure water, which has often been associated with the water of Christian baptism! Yet the washing of the body and clothes in pure water held a spiritual significance long before in Hebrew worship (Ex. 19:10; Lev. 14:8–9; Ps. 51:1–2; 7–10). Elisha, son of Shaphat, poured water onto the hands of Elijah (2 Ki. 3:11). the pure water that signified the sanctifying power of the Holy Spirit of God (Jn. 1:33)! Even in New Testament times, orthodox Jews practised the '*Mikvah*', a ceremonial double immersion in ice cold water for converts to Judaism, proving their rebirth to a new life in this world and the next!

John the Baptist used this Hebraic rite and modified its significance by preaching confession and repentance for the forgiveness of sins (Mk. 1:4). But Jesus was baptised by John, even when born without sin and remaining sinless throughout his incarnation. Even so, there are many alternative explanations for Jesus insisting on being baptised by water, when the Spirit of God descended upon him. First and foremost, it was to proclaim the beginning of his worldly ministry and the saving power of his heavenly Father. Secondly, he was acknowledging the divine authority of the Old Covenant and the last of its prophets (John the Baptist). Last but not least, he may have wished to draw attention to his human nature, which enabled him to sympathise with his follower's struggle against their inherent sin!

Later, John the Baptist declared that Jesus would supersede his baptism by baptising his followers with the Holy Spirit and fire. In a pre-ascension address the risen Lord commanded the disciples to baptise all in the name of the Father and of the Son and of the Holy Spirit (Mt. 28:19). Therefore this command was more likely to refer to a spiritual baptism of faith, symbolising the reality of salvation through a personal belief in Christ's death, burial and resurrection (Ro. 6:3–4). Therefore, baptism into Christian living is a declaration of faith, whether or not symbolised by the submersion or sprinkling of water! Paul states that Christ gave himself for the church, that he might sanctify and cleanse it with the washing of water through the word (Eph. 5:25–26).

Then follows the two commands (Heb. 10:22–23)!

First Command

"Let us draw near to God with a sincere heart in full assurance of faith."

This invitation is for all believers to draw near to God's most holy presence in the sanctuary through the blood-covenant forged between him and our Saviour. This is the pattern of true prayer, presenting favourable circumstances for God's people to worship. As God our heavenly Father is Spirit, let us worship him in the Spirit and truth (Jn. 4:24). Communion with the heavenly Father is available through the full assurance of faith in our High Priest's ability to save by the power of his atoning sacrifice. The Lord Jesus Christ is able to secure an entry for believers in daily prayer, when our sinful hearts are covered by his righteousness!

Second command

"Let us hold unswervingly to the hope we profess, for he who promised is faithful."

It is for us to hold constantly to the hope we possess, which is the promise of eternal life in this world and the next. We like Solomon will always find God faithful (2 Chr. 6:14).

This is our greatest possession, the driving force in our Christian living and service. Whatever the challenge and however dark the way before us, there is the burning belief in God who is faithful and promises the reward of eternal life. For his love, compassion and mercy follow us throughout our lives (Ps. 23:6; Isa. 43:1–4; Jas. 5:11). This final point of encouragement in the apostolic appeal was to underline the truth that their new High Priest was ever faithful!

During his last imprisonment, when shackled in a cold dungeon, the Apostle wrote in his last letter to Timothy:

"I have fought the good fight. I have finished the race. I have kept the faith.
Now there is in store for me the crown of righteousness,
which the Lord, the righteous judge, will award me on that day –
and not only for me, but also to all who have longed for his appearing."
(2 Tim. 4:7–8)

God has confirmed on oath his promise of eternal life for those who believe in his Son (Jn. 1:12). As Moses taught their forefathers, *Yahweh* could neither lie, nor deny himself, for he is the unchanging living God. Later, our heavenly Father proved his faithfulness by offering up his only Son for our salvation.

After Christ's atoning sacrifice had been completed, his heavenly Father awarded him honour and distinction, by making him our great High Priest and mediator between God's holiness and our sinful nature. The proof of the fulfilment of this promise was Christ's resurrection, as the first-born of many who believe, to bring his people from death into life. God also rewards them for their faith in Christ, by promising to share his very presence through a personal entry into the sanctuary of the paradisiacal Tabernacle prepared for them before the world began!

Such privileges cannot fail to stimulate a love (*agape*) for God and also for our fellow believers. We are encouraged by sharing the peace of our Lord Jesus with them and also by our good works. As we are members of one body, partaking of one loaf, our affection is displayed by sharing the sacraments with one another, for the Day of his return is fast approaching (Mt. 24:13; Lk. 21:8–12,34; Jas. 5:8).

These last commands are reminiscent of many of the Apostle Paul's previous letters (Ro. 5:1–5;1 Cor. 13:13; Gal. 5:5–6; Col. 1:4–5 and 1 The. 1:3). especially his letter to the church in Corinth, in which he quotes the same tripod of faith, hope and love. This refers to our faith in the saving power of the risen Lord, the hope of eternal life through belief in the purchasing power of the Holy Spirit. Finally, there is the unfailing love of our heavenly Father who in return commands us to love one another (Ro. 13:9–10).

9. Final Appeal

The penultimate chapter of this epistle includes one last appeal to the wavering Jewish converts, which is preceded by a final warning from the Apostle concerning the discipline of the Triune God. It is a concluding message of encouragement, to hold fast to their newfound profession of Christian faith and not to be tempted to return to their previous belief in Judaism. For the Gospel of Christ is full of grace and truth; this is of immeasurable superiority compared to the uncompromising severity of the Mosaic Law.

Firstly, the Apostle warns that a heavenly crowd of witnesses is watching over them. These were early Hebrew martyrs, who firmly based the foundations of their faith on the promises of *Yahweh*. They set an example for others to follow, by testifying to the power of their belief that emanated from the faithfulness of their God.

Secondly, the author states that life in this world is comparable to running a long-distance race with perseverance, only to be won by jettisoning the enthralment of sin. This is another hallmark of Paul's previous teaching of faith,

"running the race to gain the crown – the eternal crown."

(1 Cor. 9:24–25)

Again the Apostle states,

"I press on to obtain the goal, to take hold of that for which Christ took hold for me – to win the prize for which God called me,"

(Php. 3:12–14)

Even later, in his letters to Timothy, he wrote,

"Fight the good fight – take hold of eternal life, to which you were called."

(1 Tim. 6:12; 2 Tim. 4:7–8)

Thirdly, they were to concentrate on their newborn belief in Jesus Christ,

"Fixing their eyes upon Jesus, the pioneer and perfecter of faith.
For the joy set before him he endured the cross, scorning the shame,
and sat down at the right hand of the throne of God."

(Heb. 12:2)

Jesus had run the same race for all believers, accepting the imputation of the sins of the world upon his innocent body. His struggle resisted to the point of shedding his precious blood, signifying his faith in the promises of his heavenly

Father (Heb. 12:4).

Finally, they were not to lose heart in their struggle, but to remember that God disciplines those he loves, as a worldly father disciplines his son. In order to enforce this belief, the Apostle reminds them of the wisdom of David and Solomon, two of the greatest kings of Israel:

"Blessed is the man you discipline, O LORD, the man you teach from your law, -
My son, do not despise the Lord's discipline and do not resent his rebuke, because the Lord disciplines those he loves, as a father the son he delights in."
(Ps. 94:12 and Pr. 3:11–12)

And the reward being that we may share his holiness, harvesting his righteousness and peace.

10. Conclusions

The Apostle ends this concluding message by providing a world-shattering illustration between the awesome experience of their forefathers in the desert, who camped near to 'the mountain of fear'; as compared to the experience of peace and tranquility of 'the spiritual mountain of joy', available to all believers in the Son of God (Heb. 12:18–24).

The first experience took place near Mount Sinai, the mountain of God. This was a tangible reality, burning with fire in a darkened world of gloom and storm. The people feared the sound of the trumpet that heralded the descent of the LORD and could not bear to hear the word spoken to them, because of what it commanded. The sight even made Moses tremble with fear. The awesomeness was complete when the foot of the mountain became untouchable, with the threat of death to any person or animal that disobeyed.

Such a scenario did not bear comparison to the second experience of being part of the joyful assembly found near to the second mountain, Mount Zion, the spiritual mountain that is eternal. For it is the city of our living God, the heavenly Jerusalem in the paradisiacal kingdom. The church is of the firstborn, whose names are written in heaven in the city of God. The Covenant Lord is the judge of all those made righteous and perfect through the atoning sacrifice of their Saviour. He is the mediator of the New Covenant, through his sprinkled blood that speaks a better word than the blood of Abel!

We have not come to the mountain that cannot be touched,

"But you have come to Mount Zion, to the heavenly Jerusalem, the city of the living God."
(Heb. 12:22)

It is important to note that we have already come! The invitation is for all believers to come immediately, as it is not referring to an experience after we have left this world! It is entirely possible, even essential, to approach this spiritual mountain in the paradisiacal kingdom of heaven in our daily worship of the triune God. By the advocacy of the Holy Spirit, whose very presence is in the hearts of all believers, one can approach the celestial throne of our Saviour in spiritual prayer. Due to his atoning sacrifice, we might even dare follow the Holy Spirit through the veil that is Christ's body into the most holy presence of the heavenly Father. For it is only there we may praise God's holy name, giving thanks for the grace that flows to us through Jesus Christ.

But there is one final warning!

"See to it that you do not refuse him who speaks – for our God is a consuming fire!"

(Heb. 12:25–29)

He offers this last chance of an eternal life in his celestial city that is still to come on earth and cannot be shaken. Therefore let us be thankful and worship God with reverence and awe!

The book of Hebrews ends with the benediction,

"May the God of peace, who through the blood of the eternal covenant brought back from the dead our Lord Jesus, that great Shepherd of the sheep, equip you with everything good for doing his will, and may he work in us what is pleasing to him, through Jesus Christ, to whom be glory for ever and ever. Amen."

(Heb. 13:20)

CHAPTER 7

CHRISTIAN FAITH

**"Without faith it is impossible to please God,
because anyone who comes to him
must believe that he exists and that he rewards
those who earnestly seek him."**
(Heb. 11:6)

1. Introduction

At the beginning of the second chapter it was said that God created mankind in his own image that he might continue to live among them, even after their fall from grace. In return for his faithfulness and grace, God hoped they would endeavour to glorify his name. Yet he realised it was necessary to provide a plan of a temporary dwelling place for his very presence in this world, which would still preserve his holiness. He also provided copies of the pattern of the 'eternal ordinances of divine worship' from the heavenly sanctuary in the paradisiacal kingdom. These divine regulations were far above anything the human mind might conceive and were the source of God's power that upheld the Mosaic-Levitical system of worship for more than a thousand years. No man-made faith has ever challenged the superiority and the devotion embodied in the first Covenant between God and mankind (Mal. 4:4). It is still admired by all God's chosen people in this modern secular world!

God selected Moses to be his chosen servant and provided

him with the authority and power to lead the Israelites. Much of the success of the Hebrew economy was due to the devotion of God's servant. Similarly, as Jesus said of John the Baptist (Mt. 11:11), none born of man and woman had ever been a greater saviour, prophet and deliverer of God's people. This statement was upheld by the supreme privilege given to Moses of being the first to be called with Elijah to the Mount of Transfiguration, to prepare the Saviour for his ultimate sacrifice (Mt. 17:3; Mk. 9:4). But these claims naturally exclude King Melchizedek and Jesus of Nazareth, as neither had a worldly father!

The failure of the first Covenant was explored in the third chapter and the promise of the second Covenant in the fifth. Habakkuk was a man of strong and robust faith. He cried out to the LORD concerning the decline of the ungodly Hebrews of Judah into wicked practices, even before the Babylonian invasion in 586 B.C. But the LORD declared to him that the revelation of his divine promise awaited an appointed time (Hab. 2:3)! The fulfilment of God's promise was summarised by the Apostle in the first four verses of Hebrews, as recorded on page 113.

Upon the divine foundation of the Old Covenant, our heavenly Father's condescension provided a new development in a believer's approach to worship under an eternal Covenant through the grace of our Lord Jesus Christ. As a reward for personal belief, Christians receive the heavenly Father's pardoning grace and the gift of his Holy Spirit, who reveals God's Word and convicts all believers of their sinful state. Divine revelation and reasoning leads to repentance and justification, this being a process of sanctification that sets the believer apart, as being holy and righteous in God's sight.

'The Sanctifier and sanctified are all one in Christ.'

(Jn. 17:19; Heb. 3:14)

Over and above the well-established Mosaic Levitical economy founded upon the Old Covenant, the superiority of Christian faith under the New Covenant is totally dependent upon God's saving grace and divine revelation. Regardless of our inherent sinfulness, we are redeemed and reconciled to God by Christ's atoning sacrifice (Ro. 3:25; Heb. 2:17). This gift of reconciliation is given to a person for their individual recognition of the power of God's Son, as Saviour and Redeemer, for those who believe are justified and saved by faith alone, through God's good grace (Ro. 4:5).

None of the world's sophistication and wisdom has contributed to the modern day Christian worship of God. The superiority of Christianity above that of orthodox Hebrew worship is dependent upon a personal belief in the power of Jesus Christ to save, as revealed in the Gospels. In the words of the Apostle Paul, belief in the crucifixion and resurrection of Christ is a stumbling block to the Jews and foolishness to the Gentile secular world; but to those whom God has called, Christ is the power and wisdom of God (1 Cor. 1:18–25).

Therefore Christian faith in the atoning sacrifice of the Lord Jesus Christ, our Saviour and Redeemer is a gift from God (Eph. 2:8). Its very essence is our belief in Christ's anguish on the cross of Golgotha, when he suffered the torments of hell to pay the price of all sin, which God had imputed upon him. His passion culminating in his death by the shedding of his precious blood redeemed all who believe and have faith in him (Php. 3:7–11). The Holy Spirit enables the believer to accept the doctrines of the cross and the resurrection of the Lord Jesus Christ,

"And if Christ has not been raised, your faith is futile; you are still in your sins."
(1 Cor. 15:17)

As Jesus instructed his followers that they should deny themselves and take up the cross and follow him (Mk. 8:34; Lk. 9:23, 14:27), it should be a requisite of Christian faith to fulfil this command by visiting Golgotha in and through spiritual worship. This command is not only fulfilled at the communion service, but also in daily prayer by worshipping our compassionate crucified Saviour and Redeemer. Such faithfulness has a direct influence over our intellect, heart, willpower and behaviour (Ps. 119:9–16).

Jesus did not attempt to reveal the divine mystery of the cross to his disciples until they had learned to recognise the very existence of God and also believe he was the Christ, the Son of God (Jn. 20:29–31). The third member of the Holy Trinity was revealed to them to be the Holy Spirit of God (Jn. 4:23–24, 14:15–17) whose unique role was to establish Christian faith in human hearts! It is therefore incumbent upon believers to acknowledge the identity of the Triune God and to know and love each member of the Trinity, as

"Faith is being sure of what we hope for and certain of what we do not see."
(Heb. 11:1)

2. The Identity of the Triune God

Therefore the supreme privilege of being able to worship God is granted only to those who believe in the divine presence of the heavenly Father and his Son. The Holy Spirit reveals the truth of the word of God to believers. They are encouraged to accept the identity of the Trinity of God and to love each Person with all their hearts. So may we begin by studying the following Scriptural truths that are generally recognised to be the non-controversial principles of our faith.

According to Apostle Paul, the gospel was made known to Abraham in advance, for he was a man of faith. All who have this faith are Abraham's spiritual seed, children of God, and heirs according to the promise of the Spirit of God (Gal. 3:6–14). It was God's Word (Jn. 1) that conveyed the divine revelation to Abraham. This can be considered an appearance or manifestation of the Covenant LORD, which not infrequently occurred at times recorded throughout Scripture. He later revealed himself to the patriarchs, Abraham, Isaac and Jacob by the Hebrew name, *El-Shadai,* being translated 'God Almighty' (Ge. 17:1).

God declared himself before Moses as, ***"I AM WHO I AM."*** and instructed him to tell the Israelites,

> ***"The LORD, the God of your fathers - has sent me to you. This is my name forever, the name you shall call me from generation to generation"***
>
> ***(Ex. 3:14-15)***

Subsequently, the Israelites worshipped the 'LORD our God', whose name became revered, glorious and awesome among them (Dt. 28:58). It was pronounced *Yahweh,* in

Hebrew, or by the old transliterated name of '*Jehovah*'. It remained God's divine covenant name by which he redeemed his people. This led to God's name becoming recognised as being not only awesome and humbling, but also sacred and too holy to be uttered by the Israelites.

King David called the LORD God, the 'Rock', my fortress, deliverer and Saviour, the God of Israel (2 Sam. 22:2 and 47). Isaiah worshipped the 'LORD Almighty' (Isa. 2:12, 9:7) the 'Sovereign LORD' (Isa. 40:10, 61:1). Jeremiah believed in the 'LORD our Righteousness,' our Righteous Saviour (Jer. 23:6)! Therefore the Old Testament declared there to be only one God (Isa. 44:6–8; Ro. 3:30) the Rock (Dt. 32:4).

In one of the earliest recordings of religious doctrines, called the '*Shema*', it is quoted,

"The LORD our God, the LORD is one.
Love the LORD your God with all your heart and
with all your soul and with all your strength."
(Dt. 6:4-9)

(These words were immortalised by Jesus, as the first and greatest commandment (Mt. 22:37).

The Hebrews and Jews believed God to be an eternal and infinite Spirit (Jn. 4:24), whose omnipresence had neither spatial, nor temporal boundaries. God was everywhere, being invisible and imperceptible. It was also believed that his eternal existence was self-sufficient, being totally supporting in power and independence. He was omniscient in having total knowledge of the past, present and future. Nevertheless, the dimensions of these divine attributes were not only humbling, but far beyond normal human reasoning. So God in his infinite wisdom decreed that his natural characteristics would be revealed in his only Son, he being Son of God and Son of Man. Born of a woman, Christ inherited a human nature that enabled him to sympathise with his people (Mt. 3:10–15; Jn. 11:35).

Therefore in Christ we find that God is love (*agape*) and is morally perfect to those who believe in him. *Yahweh* is also awesome and humbling, gentle and kind; holy yet gracious; righteous but merciful. The New Testament enhanced this fundamental faith by defining a Trinitarian doctrine concerning the Godhead, co-equal and co-eternal in power and glory (Mt. 28:19; Ac. 2:17–18; and 2 Cor. 13:14).

The concept of the Holy Trinity revealed God the Father to be a divine Creator, reaching out to his chosen people in and through two Advocates, God the Son being the divine Redeemer and God the Holy Spirit the divine Sanctifier. This Scriptural revelation of the Triune God declares a fundamental belief expressed in the Creed, which is believed to be of apostolic testimony. Three hundred years later, it was followed by the 'Nicene Creed', in which a third fundamental doctrine of Christian faith was introduced (*see* Appendix). This was based on the New Testament concept of the Trinity, which is to be found in an enlightened form in modern editions of the Book of Common Prayer:

'The Holy Spirit, who with the Father and the Son together is worshipped and glorified.'

God The Father

According to Scripture, men and women were created for the one purpose of dedicating their lives to reflecting the glory of the Creator God. (Isa. 43:1–13). This goal is attained through faith, worship and service, creating a divine relationship through knowing God the heavenly Father. This intimate knowledge of him is gained through a personal acquaintance with his Son, who is the image and the exact representation of his heavenly Father (Col. 1:15 and Heb. 1:3, K.J.V.).

Therefore the Father reveals himself through his Son that we might follow him and come to know of his love by trusting and obeying his commands (Jn. 14:23–24). Such divine knowledge is acquired through the Holy Spirit's revelation of Scriptural truth. He prepares believers for this personal fulfilment through the process of sanctification, by worshipping God and also by witnessing to an ongoing process of being 'set apart' from the secular world in thought, word and deed.

God The Son

Before our Lord's advent, the Jews referred to their future deliverer as the 'Anointed One' in preference to the title of 'Messiah'. They believed he would be the Son of God, a celestial being higher than the angels. According to their prophets, he would assume a human form to become a great Saviour (Act. 1:6). As Moses their first deliverer had led their forefathers out of Egypt, they hoped and believed his successor would restore the unity of the divided kingdom of Israel. Such an achievement could only be attained through the power of his personal righteousness, without him suffering an expiatory death!

In retrospect the Hebrew race were wrong in not being prepared to accept the truth in the prophetic revelations from God, as revealed in Old Testament Scripture. Yet the majority were blinded from seeing the doctrinal truth of the

Messiah's advent (Isa. 6:9–10; Jn. 12:39–41) as fulfilled by Jesus Christ (Mt. 23:37–39; Lk. 13:34,19:41).

Scripture relates how the eternal Son of God became incarnate (Jn. 1:14) being born of God and a virgin called Mary, who was told to name her first-born Jesus (Lk. 1:31); the command was repeated to Joseph, to whom she was espoused (Mt. 1:20–21). Subsequently, this God-man lived a sinless life, preaching and fulfilling the will of his heavenly Father. Yet the world crucified him! He died a sacrificial death by the shedding of his precious blood, to become the Saviour of all on whom God's favour rests (Lk. 2:14).

Faith

Therefore by listening to the word of God, those chosen to believe become sheep in his flock (Jn. 10:16). They are given a secure belief in Jesus Christ, a rebirth that is essentially the first step of salvation in Christian faith. Justification by faith is always the reward of God's saving grace.

But there is this second step to be taken by all believers in order to gain a living faith by embracing Jesus. This involves recognition of Christ's subservience to the cross as our Saviour and also the magnitude of his atoning sacrifice as our Redeemer (Ro. 8:17). The heavenly Father gave the highest reward to his Son for his faithfulness by raising his body from the grave and appointing him to be above all creation, as the risen Lord Jesus Christ (Php. 2:6–11).

Whereas all Christians acknowledge Jesus Christ to be their saving and redeeming Lord and the debt owed to him for his atoning sacrifice, an even more intimate revelation is given to those chosen to dedicate their lives to his service (Php. 1:29).They become most precious to the Father and to the Son. Their personal sacrifice is the third and final step to be taken, following on the recognition of the inexpressible cost paid by Christ. It demands a new life, which requires the humility that imparts blessedness through continual spiritual baptism into the life of Christ. This is the last stage in the process of sanctification in this world, its peace with God depending upon the personal acknowledgement of the total cost paid by our Redeemer (Jn. 13:10–11).This divine title is inseparable from the Cross; for each is the rubric of the enormous price that Christ paid, as a ransom for our sins and the guarantor of eternal life in the celestial kingdom of the Triune God.

God The Holy Spirit

Following Christ's ascension into heaven, God sent the Holy Spirit to be another co-equal and divine advocate, to live forever in the hearts of all believers. When justified by faith, Christians are anointed with the Holy Spirit, as a gift from the Father (Ps. 21:5; Eze. 36:27; Ro. 5:5; 2 Cor. 1:22 and Gal. 4:6). The Holy Spirit provides a new approach to prayer, which is included in the 'latter regulation of worship' for all believers. This involves a spiritual elevation, to enable an entry into the divine presence of the Son and through his mediation into the most holy presence of the Father. The doctrine of the Holy Spirit reveals his power to raise the worshipper to these heavenly realms (Eze. 3:14, 8:3; 2 Cor. 12:2) to participate in true worship (Eph. 1:3, 20).

Another vital role of the Holy Spirit is to reveal the truth of God through his written word found in the Old and New Testaments, their understanding being dependent upon one another. The Apostle Paul declares this role, using the old Hebraic custom of sealing (Dt. 32:34).

"And you were also included in Christ when you heard the word of truth, the gospel of your salvation. Having believed, you were marked in him with a seal, the promised Holy Spirit, who is a deposit guaranteeing our inheritance until the redemption of those who are God's possession – to the praise of his glory"

(Eph. 1:13–14).

Yet there are some believers who do not appear to be fully prepared to recognise the personhood and the sanctifying power of the Holy Spirit in their daily worship. They reveal an aura of uneasiness in acknowledging and declaring his power to transform their faith, leading to repentance and subsequently to a spiritual worship of God. Yet Scripture declares,

'This Spirit of Grace is a divine Person, co-equal with the heavenly Father and with the Son: God in Three Persons; blessed Trinity.'
(Dr. M. Lloyd-Jones.).

Whereas the majority of evangelical Christians pray to the Father and to the Son, only a minority appear to be prepared to pray directly to the Holy Spirit. However, all believers must learn never to detract from the glory of the third Person.

'He is not just an influence, not some 'It'. He is indeed God the Holy Spirit.' (Dr. M. Lloyd-Jones)

Throughout Scripture the Holy Spirit's presence and power are referred to as living water! The Old Testament mentions the water from the wells of salvation and a spring that never fails. (Isa. 12:3, 58:11) In the New Testament, Jesus promised the Samaritan woman that he would give her a spring of living water, welling up to eternal life! Later, at the Feast of Tabernacles, he promised those who believe in him would gain rivers of living waters within them (Jn. 4:10–14; 7:37–38).

The chief role of this 'giver of life' within the Holy Trinity is to glorify the Son. He fulfils this work of grace in a very prolific manner, by making known to believers the knowledge he receives from the heavenly Father through the risen Lord (Jn. 16:14–15; 1 Cor. 12:3).

It is therefore of prime importance for all believers to be aware of the power of the Holy Spirit and treat him as an intimate friend, never grieving him, nor quenching his personal guidance in our Christian lives and worship. To prevent falling into this dilemma, we should pray in the Spirit on all occasions (Ro. 8:26–27; Eph. 6:18). One can only pray in and through the Holy Spirit at all times by praying to him and acknowledging his continuous presence within our hearts! In this way, he concentrates and influences our thoughts and the content of our prayers.

Following Paul's instruction, Aurelius Augustine and David Martyn Lloyd-Jones recorded two great examples of this revelation. The evidence for this statement can be found in the Appendix, which contains two of their favourite meditations.

3. The Word of God (*dubar*. Heb.)

"In the beginning was the Word,
the Word was with God,
and the Word was God.
The same was in the beginning with God."
(Jn. 1:1. K.J.V.)

Scripture records the Word of the LORD came to Abram in a vision, promising to be his shield. It was also promised that he would have a son, whose offspring would be more numerous than the stars in the heavens. Although being one hundred years old and married to a barren wife, *"Abram believed the LORD and he credited it to him as righteousness" (Ge. 15:1–6).* Abram's reward was given for his faith in the words of the LORD and not for his good works (Ro. 4:1–4).

Later God spoke to Moses from a bush on fire and commanded him to go to Pharaoh and bring his people out of Egypt! Moses believed and obeyed the LORD and eventually became a great servant of God (Ex. 4:15). Subsequently he was called to the summit of Mount Sinai to be given the words of the LORD; they were written in stone by the finger of God! As in all covenants, there was the original agreement and a copy, one for each participant. Moses gave the two tablets to the people and ordered them to write the Commandments upon their hearts (Dt. 6:6). God's people came to treasure these Testaments and preserved them in the Ark of the Covenant.

It is recorded in the Psalms that all God's words are true and all his righteous laws are eternal (Ps. 119:160), perfect and refreshing to the soul; they are trustworthy and give joy to the heart; they are radiant and give light to the eyes; they are more precious than gold and sweeter than honey. By keeping them there is great reward (Ps. 19:7–11).

The Book of Proverbs is filled with the 'sayings of the wise' and the wisdom of God. Wisdom is personified as a manifestation of the LORD (Pr. 1:20–33, 3:13–18). Later, the wisdom of God is linked to the word of God, both being attributes of the LORD, the firstborn of his creation and constantly existing at his side before and during the creation of the world (Pr. 8:22–31).

In the New Testament, God's Word is given the Greek term of *Logos*, as in Theo–logos or Theology. Greek philosophers used it in reference to the wisdom or reasoning and in the spoken word emanating from all divine powers governing the universe. It corresponds to the wisdom and the spoken word, which reveals the thoughts of God. The doctrine of St. John identified the Logos to be the personification of the Son of God, who existed before the creation of the world and was made incarnate as Jesus of Nazareth. He was the supreme manifestation of God's Wisdom and his Word (1 Cor. 1:30; Col. 2:3).

"All things were made by him:
and without him was not anything made that was made."
"In him was life: and that life was the light of men.
And the light shineth in darkness: and the darkness comprehended it not -
That was the true Light, which lighteth every man that cometh into the world."
(Jn. 1:3–5 and 9 K.J.V.)

Jesus claimed to be the light of the world. He promised those who follow him will never walk in darkness, but will have the light of life (Jn. 8:12).

Jesus also declared:

"I am the bread of life. Whoever comes to me
will never go hungry,
and whoever believes in me will never be thirsty."
"I am the living bread that came down from
heaven.
Whoever eats of this bread will live forever.
This bread is my flesh, which I will give for the
life of the world."
(Jn. 6:35 and 51)

Previously, when tempted by the devil in the wilderness, Jesus answered,

"It is written: Man does not live on bread alone,
but on every word that comes from the mouth
of God."
(Dt. 8:3; Mt. 4:4)

At the Last Supper Jesus took bread, gave thanks and broke it and gave it to his disciples, saying,

"This is my body given for you; do this in
remembrance of me."
(Lk. 22:19; 1 Cor. 11:23–26)

**"And the Word was made Flesh and dwelt among us,
and we beheld his glory, the glory as of the only begotten of the Father,
full of grace and truth**

(Jn. 1:14. K.J.V.)

Today, believers accept Holy Scripture in the Bible to be the infallible word of God. It provides the food by which we live and grow (Dt. 30:14; Jn. 6:33; 1 Pe. 2:2) being truthful (Ps. 119:160) and pure (Pr. 30:5). It keeps us from sin (Ps. 119:11), cleanses (Jn. 15:3; Eph. 5:26) and sanctifies us in the sight of God (Jn. 17:17). It is the means of our faith (Ac. 6:7; Ro. 10:17).

"Seek ye out the book of the LORD and read!"

(Isa. 34:16. K.J.V.)

4. The Kingdom of Heaven – God's Kingly Rule

'It is in particular to the Hebrew people that we owe the most ineradicable belief that the Deity lives above.' (Harmsworth).

The Israelites believed in heaven being God's dwelling place, but his omniscience gave him the power to live and reign over his covenant people, a kingdom of priests and a holy nation. (Ge. 18:18–19; Ex. 19:6; Isa. 57:15) His kingship or kingly rule had no end, neither spatially nor temporally, as declared by the prophet (Isa. 52:7). It is recorded in the Old Testament that when the Israelites pleaded with Samuel for him to anoint an earthly king to lead the nation in battle, he pointed out to them that the LORD their God was their king and had led them successfully against their enemies (1 Sam. 12:13–15). So the concept of a heavenly king, or the sovereignty and rule of God over all of his created order was subsequently engraved on the hearts of all Israel.

The titles of the 'kingdom of heaven' and the 'kingdom of God' never appeared in the Old Testament, although the concept eventually became recognised by the Jews (Mt. 3:2). But they were the main feature of the Gospel of Jesus Christ, who became acknowledged to be the kingdom in person. Whereas the disciples were given the key to the mysteries of the kingdom, the Saviour used the language of parables (Ps. 78:1–2) to withhold from non-believers the fact that God's reign was radically different from the human concept of an all-powerful kingly rule.

There has never been a more forceful and decisive communicator compared to Jesus of Nazareth, who repeatedly used parables as a figurative form of speech. They expressed imagination and feeling, a form of speech in which the abstract was clothed in reality, as they included an overt moral application and a hidden spiritual meaning.

There were more than thirty parables recorded in the Synoptic Gospels, at least six revealing the divine secrets of the kingly rule of heaven and of God. There were two concerning vineyards, which was not surprising, as there are 243 references to wine in the Bible dating back to Noah (Ge. 9:21). Both parables were in reference to the vineyard God had planted in the Promised Land, in which the people were being likened to the vines (Isa. 5:7).

In the 'Parable of the Two Sons' (Mt. 21:28–32) the father who owned the vineyard asked the first to go and work for him; initially he refused, but later changed his mind and obeyed. In the meanwhile, the father asked the second son to go; he said, "I will, Sir", but did not go!

Jesus told this parable to the chief priest and elders of the Temple, whom he likened to the second son, because they did not recognise his gospel of light to the world, as John proclaimed later (Jn. 1:9)! So they were being informed that the sinful tax collectors and prostitutes were ahead of them as his chosen people, because they had accepted his way of righteousness and consequently the door of repentance remained open for them to enter the 'kingdom of God.'

The second 'Parable of the Tenants (Mt. 21:33–41) was about cruel men employed by the owner to take care of the same vineyard, but they wished to take possession and were deceitful towards their master. They killed every servant sent to collect the fruit and eventually murdered his son, whom he expected them to respect! This was an overt judgement upon the Chief Priests and Pharisees, who had persecuted and killed God's prophets in the past and were then plotting to kill his only Son. Jesus was warning them that the 'kingdom of God' would be taken away from them and given to people who showed their respect for the heavenly Father and his Son by producing plenty of fruit for their owner!

As his followers became accustomed to this form of teaching, the parables became similar in type to the Old Testament prophecies in that they contained a double telescopic view of contemporary and distant revelations. This is not surprising, as Jesus was our greatest prophet.

In the 'Parables of the Mustard Seed and the Yeast' (Mt. 13:31–33; Mk. 4:30–32; Lk. 13:18–20) Jesus compared the miraculous growth of a tiny seed and the spread of the yeast throughout the flour and dough in bread making, to the growth and spread of the power of the kingly rule of God, when first conceived in the hearts of all believers through the presence of the Holy Spirit.

The 'Parable of the Wedding Banquet' (Mt.22:1–14; Lk.14:16–24) was the story of a king who had prepared a feast for his son's wedding and invited all his friends, but they refused to come for some trivial reasons. So in his anger the father sent his servants to invite anyone they could find on the streets – the poor, crippled, blind and lame!

According to the custom, on arrival the guests washed away the dust from their journey and were offered clean wedding garments before coming to the banquet table. But the king noticed that one man had scorned his host's courtesy and was wearing his own soiled clothes. His host asked him for the reason, but ashamedly he had none. Consequently he was ejected from the room for insulting his host! The first guests invited were the Jewish people, who had no respect for the Son of God. And those who took their places represented the Gentiles who readily accepted Christ's invitation.

"He came unto his own and his own received him not!"

(Jn. 1:11. K.J.V.)

Luke records the same parable, but related it to the table of a rich Pharisee (Lk.14:15).One of his Hebrew guests pointedly referred to the blessing of those invited to the feast in the kingdom of God. The Jews boasted that this was their privilege, as they alone were sufficiently righteous to attend the great eschatological Messianic banquet in the future kingdom, having been given God's Law – the Sepher Torah (Isa. 25:6).

But Jesus taught that this great feast was in the kingdom of God. It not only symbolised the future intimate relationship between God and his people, but also a communion that is spiritually attainable to all believers in their worship during their lives in this world (Lk. 22:16).

"For the wedding of the Lamb has come,
and his bride (the Church) has made herself ready.
Fine linen, bright and clean,
was given to her to wear."
(Rev. 19:7–8)

Therefore, it appears in retrospect, Jesus was teaching the Pharisees that the two essential hallmarks of Christian faith are a deep respect for the Son of God and his humility. This was recorded in the wonderful words of the Apostle Paul in his letter to the Church of Philippi, in which he advised them to imitate Christ's humility (Php. 2:6–11).

The ungrateful guest in the parable, who was not prepared to accept the customary hospitality before entering the royal presence, could well represent worshippers who are not contrite enough to be clothed in Christ's 'garments of humility and righteousness'. This is an essential step of faith for worshippers, before attempting to prayerfully enter into the most holy presence of the heavenly Father (Mt. 23:12)!

The 'Parable of the Ten Virgins' (Mt. 25:1-13) is the story of ten virgins who were waiting to greet the bridegroom. There were five who were foolish in taking only their lamps and not remembering to take any extra oil for replenishment. The remaining five were wiser in taking not only their lamps, but also extra oil in jars. This enabled them to trim their lamps, in the event of having to wait a longer time for the bridegroom to arrive. By then the foolish virgin's lamps had gone out and they were forced to go and find extra oil, whereas the wise virgins were able to keep their lamps trimmed and were prepared to receive him. They were invited to go with him into the wedding banquet, but then the door was shut and the foolish virgins were refused entry! Therefore the overt warning was to be prepared and keep watching, because one never knows the day or the hour that the keeper of the kingdom will appear at his future return!

The Parable of the Narrow Door, or the 'Strait Gate of Humiliation', referred to the time when Jesus was asked whether only a few people might be saved! He replied that there would always be a careful selection of those allowed entry into the kingdom of God! So he urged his followers to make every effort to enter life through the narrow door of humility. Many will try otherwise, but would be unable to gain entry. Some might even boast of knowing the owner of the house, but he will answer, "I don't know you, or where you come from!"(Lk. 13:24–30).

Jesus had said previously, "Not everyone who says to me, 'Lord, Lord,' will enter the kingdom of heaven, but only he who does the will of my Father who is in heaven" (Mt. 7:21). Later, John the Apostle recorded in his Prologue, entitled, 'The Word Became Flesh',

"But as many as received him, to them gave he the power to become children of God, Even to them that believe on his name. Which were born, not of blood, nor of the will of the flesh, nor of the will of man, but of God."

(Jn. 1:12-13. K.J.V.)

5. Conclusions

These parables reveal the divine features of God's kingly rule and sovereignty over the whole of his created order on earth, as in heaven above where his most holy presence exists and where he reigns supremely. Under the Old Covenant the LORD's terrestrial rule was to be found in the sanctuary of the tabernacle and later in the temple. Under the New Covenant, Jesus of Nazareth represented God's rule on earth during his worldly pilgrimage.

Hendriksen defined the physical 'structures' from the spiritual 'presence' of God, in that the former symbolized the latter! The tabernacle and temple were the 'type' being inseparable from Christ's body that was the 'antitype', in that both were destructible; whereas the spiritual presence of God was indestructible in each! Therefore when Christ was crucified, the temple and its entire culture ceased to have any meaning; also the terrible crime of nailing him to the cross resulted in the destruction of Jerusalem with its physical temple!

After his crucifixion and ascension into heaven, the exalted Christ reigned as head of his kingly rule over the paradisiacal kingdom of heaven. Then the Holy Spirit was given eschatological powers to shape and nurture the future Messianic kingdom. He was sent to represent Christ's rule within the hearts of all believers. Although the church was commissioned to preach the Gospel of the kingdom, Jesus did not equate it with his kingship. Yet he promised it would become a sign and servant of the kingdom, when fully acknowledging his Gospel. On his return, Christ will bring his heavenly reign and will rule over the earth eternally (Mt. 16:27–28). He also prophesied that his future Church would be made up of citizens of the kingdom of heaven on earth!

Therefore, for the present, God's kingly rule is to be found in the paradisiacal Sanctuary of the celestial realms. It is approachable to all who believe in the holiness of the Father and Son and abide by their laws. They are forbidden to enter God's holy presence informally with familiarity, as none are self-righteous enough to be considered acceptable in God's sight. To attend the wedding super in the kingdom of heaven (Rev. 19:7). it is necessary for Christ to cover their sinfulness with the garments of purity, humility and righteousness through his mediating power!

As we have a great priest in heaven, appointed over God's celestial sanctuary, everything is to be committed through him. This includes former and latter regulations of worship, both being copies of the eternal 'ordinances of divine worship' given to Moses on the mountain. In this world, only Christ provides a believer with the confidence to enter the Most Holy Place of the heavenly sanctuary through his atoning sacrifice (Heb. 8:1–5. *see* page 118). By this new and living way, an entry is opened up through the curtain of Christ's body. The supreme privilege of entry is given only to sanctified sinners, so they may enter his courts with thanksgiving and praise, as they approach the Most Holy Place in which God dwells!

It has previously been suggested (page 126) that the risen Christ carried his human nature into the Heaven of Heavens, establishing an approach to God the Father for the saints to follow in his footsteps. If these concepts were true, the divine promise would be confined to glorified believers after the completion of their redemption and glorification in the paradisiacal kingdom. But Jesus promised all those who believe in him would see the kingdom of God before they die (Lk. 9:27)! He assured his disciples that their heavenly Father had already given them this right of entry into the paradisiacal kingdom, to store their treasures in heaven (Lk. 12:32–34).

Finally, the construction of the Mosaic tabernacle imposed a three-step 'former regulation of worship' upon the Israelites. In relation to this original command, a promise was made relating to a better hope, to be revealed following the replacement of the temple and first covenant (Heb. 7:18–19, 9:8). Yet under the 'latter regulations' of the new eternal covenant, the inherent sinful nature continues to affect everyone, which even includes the hearts of all believers. This means there can be no fundamental change in our spiritual relationship to the heavenly Father, as previously existed between him and the Israelites. For no person in this world, even the most righteous believer, has the privilege to enter the Father's most holy presence without an advocate and mediator, Jesus Christ. God's great condescension was to provide his only Son to be the holy sacrificial Lamb for our atonement, a ransom for reconciliation (Ex. 25:22; Lev. 16:2). The Son of God chose to be our mediator and his Holy Spirit was appointed to be our advocate.

These fundamental principles, when accepted, establish the foundation for Christian faith expressed in prayer

(Jas. 5:13–16).They are the essence of the 'latter regulation of worship' for all believers in their personal prayers to the Triune God. Therefore in this form of true worship, the Holy Spirit raises believers into Christ's very presence in the paradisiacal kingdom of heaven. This is to be found in the celestial Tabernacle, not made by human hands (Eph. 1:3). They are enabled to enter Christ's gate of salvation (Jn. 10:9) with praise, and through his mediation (Heb. 9:15) give thanks to the heavenly Father (Ps. 100:4; Heb. 13:15).

CHAPTER 8

THE DEVELOPMENT OF CHRISTIAN LITURGY

1. Introduction

It has been seen in the Old Testament that it is God's prerogative to reveal himself only to men and women he has chosen; their response to his awesome presence is through worship and service! A personal faith trusting in Christian worship is founded upon a believer's knowledge of God. Martin Luther claimed that to know God is to worship him. A small part of this knowledge is gained through observing his creation (Ps. 19:1–6), but a far greater revelation is acquired through Scripture that is God's written word (Ps. 19:7–11).

From early days believers have overcome their fear of God by gathering together in corporate worship, as did the Israelites on Mount Sinai when they trembled to hear his voice. God's condescension was to provide them with Scripture, in which Moses first recorded in the Torah or Scroll. It meant they could hear, memorise and repeat the word of God. This led to its fulfilment from a copy of the divine regulation of worship, which was handed to Moses to be practised in the tabernacle and later in the temple. When these blessings were linked to their traditional beliefs, it helped them to develop a pattern of worship. This was both covenantal and sacrificial, as it included sin-offerings to remove the barrier between them and God and also peace offerings to maintain harmony with their Creator. Therefore the balance of worship was mainly dependent upon the hearing of God's word (the Sepher Torah), accompanied by the lesser forms of traditional rites.

"For the foolishness of God is wiser than human wisdom,
and the weakness of God is stronger than human strength."
(1 Cor. 1:25)

But the human trend to ignore this Pauline text, based on the Old Testament Hebrew form of worship, has tended to repeat itself throughout the history of the church!

2. Hebrew Worship

Over the next thousand years the Israelites acquired a form of worship in their Hebrew and Aramaic tongues in the tabernacle and in the temple. During the exile, all corporate worship was banished and they became dependent upon personal individual prayer (Dan. 9:3–19).

After the exile and the rebuilding of the temple in Jerusalem, their corporate worship was revived and became very elaborate. It combined sacrifices with psalms and liturgical prayers that expressed adoration, thanksgiving and forgiveness. They employed choirs and musical instruments with processions and dancing! Therefore their traditional rites came to overshadow the Scriptural elements in their worship!

Inter-testamental Period

During the period from 433 to 5 B.C. the Hebrew liturgy in the temple and synagogues gradually changed with the replacement of sacrificial worship by the repetition of psalms and prayers. This was partly brought about by the oppression suffered during the captivity, which was ended with the conquest of Babylon by Alexander the Great and the Persian armies in 330 B.C. The subsequent occupation of the Holy Land and Egypt prepared the way for the pre-Christian translation of the Hebrew Old Testament (the Sepher Torah) into Greek. In 250 B.C. the *Septuagint* (Latin. LXX. 70) was provided as Scripture for the use of Jews that had been persuaded to live in Alexandria. Originally, it contained the first five books of Moses, but later included the remainder of the Old Testament canonical books to which some non-canonical books were added. Soon the LXX became acknowledged as the Bible of the Jews throughout the Greek-speaking world outside Israel.

3. Early Christian Worship

It was probably during the early part of his ministry, when Jesus' disciples came to recognise the importance of prayer and the influence that it had on his divine pilgrimage. They saw how their master arose before dawn to seek privacy in the mountains for prayers to his heavenly Father. Sometimes he would spend the whole night praying! Eventually, Luke records, they summoned up the courage to confront him with the words chosen to entitle this monograph, "Lord, teach us to pray, just as John (the Baptist) taught his disciples" (Lk. 11:1). In response to their request, Jesus taught them the precious words that have since become recognised as the 'Lord's Prayer'. They have been described by Saint Augustine and Martin Luther as the most wonderful passage in the whole of Scripture! Yet, in retrospect it is believed that the Lord did not intend it to be a true prayer, but a model form, as it consisted of a list of divine principles on which to build all prayers. They include recollection, invocation, adoration and petition (*see* The Lord's Prayer, page 205).

During his life in this world, Jesus set an example to support the power of personal worship with the heavenly Father (Mt. 6:6). When he met the Samaritan woman at Jacob's well, he told her that the time was coming when you will worship (corporately) neither on this mountain, nor in Jerusalem; as true worshippers must come to worship (personally) the Father in Spirit and in truth within their own hearts (Jn. 4:21–24, 14:6).

After the crucifixion, the risen Lord Jesus Christ created his early church when he breathed on his disciples and said, "Receive the Holy Spirit" (Jn. 20:22–23). Fifty days later, on the day of Pentecost, the Holy Spirit descended to fulfil the prophecy of Joel (Ch. 2:28–32). After Peter's revelation of the fulfilment of Joel's prophecy, about three thousand were added to the Church and continued as the fellowship of the believers in corporate worship (Ac. 2:14–36, 42–47).

Thus the word of God spread and the early Christian Church in Jerusalem grew rapidly in numbers (Ac. 6:7). Yet the Jews continued to attend the temple and joined in Levitical worship, accepting the Hebrew traditional rites of water baptism and the Passover meal. The latter eventually became recognised as the Last Supper rites in remembrance of Jesus breaking the bread, followed by a meal before partaking of the cup of wine to prophesy his imminent death. Subsequently the disciples used this pattern of worship at Christ's request, to recollect the atoning sacrifice of their Saviour (1 Cor. 11:23–26).

After the martyrdom of Stephen, the Hebrew priesthood persecuted the early church causing them to scatter throughout Judea, Galilee and Samaria. Saul of Tarsus was a great protagonist in this scourge, but following his conversion on the road to Damascus, he and Barnabas toiled to strengthen the early church in Damascus and later in Jerusalem (Ac. 9:31). This was achieved by increasing the number of Jewish converts and also by Peter's influence over the acceptance of Gentiles into their fellowship (Ac. 10:45; 11:18). Their corporate worship was founded upon Scripture and oral tradition; the former consisted of the Septuagint with fragments of the Synoptic Gospels written by the apostles in Greek; their regulation of worship came to include the breaking of bread and prayers.

James, the brother of Jesus, became the leader of the Jewish Christian church in Jerusalem and probable author of the letter to the scattered Christian converts. It contained advice concerning Christian behaviour, faith and service and the regulations of worship in the prayer of faith (Ja. 5:13–16). It has already been seen in Chapter 6 that Saint Paul wrote to the dissidents of the early Church concerning the regulations of worship. He recalled the structure of the earthly sanctuary and explained that the Holy Spirit was showing by its construction that the true pattern of worship had not then been disclosed, as long as the first tabernacle was still functioning. This was an illustration to them that the 'former regulation of worship' in the Old Covenant was only meant to apply until the time of a new order. He then went on to explain that this new order of worship was through Christ. He was the High Priest and mediator of the New Covenant, with its 'latter regulation of worship' (Heb. 9:1–28).

There was a thirty to forty-year delay after Christ's crucifixion before the appearance of a collection of New Testament Scripture. These were founded on the common oral tradition with written fragments, hymns and documents that preserved the various events of the life of Jesus. Although the original canonical apostolic scripts appear to have been lost, it is fortunate that much of their contents were included in subsequent manuscripts written during the second and third centuries including those of Irenaeus, Tertullus, Tatian and Origen.

4. The Church of Rome

The martyrdom of Peter and Paul in Rome appeared to strengthen the resolve of their respective disciples or followers to survive persecution. The decision over the primacy of the two Apostles was probably influenced by the Saviour's pronouncement over Peter, concerning the future of his church (Mt. 16:16–19; Jn. 21:15–19). But the debate over his successors (the Papacy) and their authority to conserve the apostolic message in Latin restricted the mission of the Christian church. This continued to cause much turmoil throughout the history of Christian witness. The evolution of Roman theology is too complex a subject to be discussed in this monograph, but the contribution of many of its converts to the revelation and preservation of Christian Scripture and worship cannot be ignored!

In 312 A.D. the Christian conversion of Constantine, the great Roman Emperor, suspended the persecution of the early Church and enhanced the spread of Christianity throughout the Western world. His mother, Queen Helena, was a Christian Jewess who persuaded her son to explore historic sites in the Holy land and restore them. They also built rotundas and increased the facilities for corporate Christian worship.

In 382 A.D. Jerome was commanded by the Papacy in Rome to compile and write a New Testament in Latin to replace previous translations of manuscripts listed above. He eventually added a revised Old Testament attempting to restrict the canon to Hebrew scripts. This research led to the completion of the first Christian Bible written in Vulgar Latin, which eventually became known as the Vulgate Bible in 1454 A.D. It remained the official version of Scripture throughout western Christian churches until 1516 A.D. Subsequently, the Roman Catholic Church retained it in revised forms and after many delays it was printed in a fully authorised edition in 1598 A.D.

At the same time, in the fourteenth century, John Wycliffe (1329–84) translated the Latin Vulgate into English. He believed that every man and woman should be able to understand the spoken or written word in their own tongue, but his attempts to spread the gospel were restricted as the printing press had not been invented! He was condemned as a heretic by the Pope and after his death the Church exhumed his body and burned it with his books in an attempt to destroy his legacy!

In 354 A.D. Augustine was born in North Africa (modern Algeria) having a very pious mother called Monnica, who taught him the principles of Christianity. Her prayers and efforts appeared to be unrewarded until her son was 33 years old. At that time he was in Milan teaching philosophy and was influenced by the preaching of Bishop Ambrose. This led him to conversion into the Catholic faith and baptism in 387 A.D.

Ambrose taught the mature Augustine how to interpret

Scripture spiritually, which persuaded him to dedicate his life to the study of theology through reasoning and faith. This led to a deep and personal understanding of the Gospel of Christ. He was influenced mainly by St. Paul's writing to the Roman Church (Ro. 7:7–25, 9:10–29), which revealed the sinfulness found in the hearts of all believers. He realised that they could only be cleansed by the atoning sacrifice of Christ, but it was God's prerogative in choosing those he wished to save by grace alone!

Augustine was appointed Bishop of Hippo in 391 A.D. He was a fluent writer and critic of the cults and false teachings that distorted the traditional rites of the early church. He defended the former regulations of the Old Testament, in believing they were the key to the understanding of the richer promises found in the New Testament, as evident in the opening quote of this monograph.

Both Catholic and Protestant believers respect St. Augustine and it is generally believed that he was one of the greatest theologians that ever lived. His teaching and instruction paved the way for the Reformation and remains a great source of biblical research. Luther appealed strictly to the authority of St. Paul and his most trustworthy interpreter St. Augustine!

Although considered to be another outstanding theologian of his time, Erasmus (1469–1536 A.D.) was not given the full recognition that he deserved, concerning his contribution to the initiation of the movement towards the Reformation. It was believed by some authorities that Erasmus lacked the courage of his convictions and it was left to Luther to establish the true word of God throughout Europe. Yet Erasmus was a frail and retiring Christian intellectual scholar, who had greater faith in the power of his pen rather than his profession and preserved a strong allegiance to the Roman Church.

Erasmus was from Rotterdam and was brought up in the Christian faith. He entered the church and was ordained as a priest at an early age in 1492, but later he studied in Paris before coming to England in 1499. There he met John Colet, who was a lecturer in Oxford at that time. Colet's teaching on the early Greek manuscripts inspired Erasmus to dedicate himself to the translation of them into Latin. This led to his understanding of the original Scriptural texts and he began to doubt the authority of the Vulgate Bible. His greatest contribution to the preservation of Scripture was the publishing of another New Testament in Latin (1516).

It was the first to be printed and was claimed to be the true Gospel of Christ. In 1532 Luther translated Erasmus' New Testament into the common language for a divided Germany.

Eventually in 1550 the Protestant Church recognised Erasmus' New Testament as the *Textus Receptus*, or the 'Received Text'. In the meantime the Roman Catholic authorities printed Jerome's Vulgate Bible in Latin. It was named the Gutenberg Bible. It was published in German nine years later and called the Mentel Bible.

In more recent times, theologians have researched many of Erasmus' works and publications. This has revealed that he had begun to criticise the Roman Church concerning its abuses of indulgences and that he initially supported Luther after the publication of his Ninety-Five Theses. Yet he could not bring himself to condone any form of rebellion against the ecclesiastical authority of Rome.

5. The Reformation

During the 15th century the Church of Rome became dominant and corrupt. Its lust for worldly power led to secularisation, exposing itself to Protestant criticism over the lack of theological instruction with its attendant spiritual poverty. Added to this, the infallibility of the Papacy became a source of dispute with theologians who supported the authority of Scripture, as compared to the traditional beliefs corrupted by the Church. But the great source of contention was the cloak of secrecy cast over the availability of Scripture to the ordinary man and woman. Rome believed in the Catholic Latin rite for translations of the Bible and that should only be made available to its clerics. They were given the exclusive authority to provide or withhold the truth of God from the laity! Such was the stimulus for change and reformation.

There were three men, Luther, Calvin and Tyndale who led the confrontation, each believing in the same truths from their individual studies of Hebrew and Greek Scripture. They became convinced that God the Father was the centre of Christian belief and his sovereign grace ensured believers of their salvation through the atoning sacrifice of his Son. He was the only mediator with the Father, whereas the Holy Spirit's hidden work convicts believers and persuades them to build their trust in the heavenly Father. Such truth was above all traditional belief!

Martin Luther was born in Saxony (Germany) in 1483. He came from a peasant background and chose a monastic life by becoming a monk and entering the Augustinian monastery in 1501. Subsequent scholastic research led to his theological professorial appointment in the University of Wittenberg in 1550. His Scriptural studies persuaded him to accept Paul's doctrine of 'justification by faith alone' (Ro. 1:17, 3:26).

This fundamental belief in God's word caused him to clash with and separate from the rulers of the Church in Rome. Following his translation of Erasmus' New Testament into German, Luther added a translation of the Hebrew Old Testament to complete the content of his Lutheran Bible.

John Calvin was born in France in 1509 and as a young scholar he became deeply influenced by Luther's publications. He studied in Paris and underwent a spiritual conversion that persuaded him to spend the rest of his life studying the Scripture and Reformation beliefs. Following his publication of the 'Institutes of Christian Religion' he was persecuted by the Church and fled to Basel and then to Geneva, where he became a powerful preacher of Protestant Christian faith. Subsequently he wrote many Latin commentaries on Scripture that were translated into French to provide the ordinary people of France a Scripture they could comprehend. Thus it was claimed that Calvin had inherited and donned Luther's mantle!

Yet Luther became recognised as the warrior monk who defied the Roman Church by his faith in the Word of God and Calvin his disciple was persuaded to believe in 'justification by grace alone'. This led to him becoming a passionate pastor and a powerful expository preacher of the Word of God. Calvin's passion for his congregation was only overshadowed by his profound love for his Saviour. He believed that every believer should have the same spiritual communion and personal encounter with the Saviour that had changed his life, as it had done to Saul on the road to Damascus more than 1500 years before (Ac. 9:3–6).

Calvin recognised Christ's historical service as prophet, priest and king, at the same time understanding the limitations of his human frailty as portrayed in Scripture. Christ's total obedience to the heavenly Father, coupled to his faithfulness towards those he loved, created a holy communion of believers. He believed that for their sake alone, Christ embraced death on the cross to provide them with an eternal life by conquering sin and replacing it with righteousness. At the same time, Calvin accepted and defended the teachings of the classical creeds, believing them to be a faithful representation of Scriptural truth based on historical facts and not mythology. He believed the historical Jesus was proof of his divinity (homoousios) and his humanity.

William Tyndale was born in England in 1494 into a land-owning Gloucestershire family. He became an outstanding scholar in Greek and Latin gaining entry into Oxford and Cambridge Universities. Like other human linguists, Tyndale mastered many languages and later taught himself Hebrew, which was almost an unknown language in England at that time.

Unlike Luther and Calvin who had to translate the old Hebrew and Greek texts into Latin, before translating the latter into their mother tongues, Tyndale was able to translate old Hebrew and Greek texts directly and fluently into English. Yet his greatest ability was to convert these translations into a neutral word order with the pattern of rhythm and sensitivity of the everyday English language. This provided a new prose using common words, which opened up the written and spoken Holy Scripture to every literate speaking Englishman and woman. It also became a method of education for the illiterate!

Above all this scholarly accomplishment, Tyndale developed a deep Christian understanding for the true Gospel of Christ in the New Testament. After returning to Gloucester, he studied the Bibles of Jerome, Erasmus and Luther, to which he added passages from his own translations of classical Hebrew and Greek texts. He met great opposition from the Roman Church in England, none greater than Thomas More who upheld Jerome's Latin Bible to be the true word of God. This led him to condemn the 'humanist movement' as blasphemous in God's sight. More believed the Protestant movement should be burnt out of England, as he considered all their followers were heretics!

Therefore Tyndale was forced to leave England in 1524 for Germany, where there were printing presses available to publish unorthodox religious books. He wrote his English New Testament in the vernacular, which became known as the 'Plough Boy Edition'. Tyndale believed that illiteracy should never be a barrier to salvation, as his Saviour had proved by choosing illiterate fishermen to be his disciples and future missionaries! His translation of the New Testament began to arrive in England during the early part of 1526. Subsequently he set about translating the Old Testament from the original text in the Pentateuch, to which he added translations of Joshua, Judges, Ruth, Samuel, Kings, Chronicles, Ezra, Nehemiah, Esther and Jonah before his martyrdom by the Church of Rome on the 6th October 1536.

Tyndale's friend and assistant, Miles Coverdale, completed his work to incorporate it into a complete English Bible. Later, Cranmer presented this Bible to Henry VIII, as being the best English edition to incorporate in the king's Great English Bible. By royal order, this was to replace the Latin Vulgate Bible that had existed in all English churches for more than a thousand years. Therefore the Great English Bible was based mainly on William Tyndale's original translations. Thus his dying wish was fulfilled, for an English Bible to be placed in every parish church throughout England!

Therefore these three great men had many things in common. They were all great scholars being fluent in Latin, Greek and even Hebrew languages. This enabled them to study the original documents and separate the contents from traditional Catholic beliefs. Such divine revelation of the supremacy of God and his activities provided a theology of God's word, which empowered them to speak with clarity through the Holy Spirit to the church and world! It has been said that Luther forced the breakthrough of the Reformation, whereas Calvin and Tyndale consolidated the Reformation by establishing the changes in their own countries!

The teaching of St. Paul and that of his disciple St. Augustine also inspired them in their crusade against the traditional beliefs and rites of the Roman Church. The 'banner of truth' was handed down by the inspiration of the Holy Spirit, first to Erasmus and then to Luther; from Luther to Calvin and from Calvin to Tyndale. This divine procession has no end, for the Holy Spirit continues to inspire those chosen by God, as revealed in the subsequent history of Church liturgy throughout the world. And it will continue to inspire men and women until the dawn of the day of Christ's promised return (Ac. 1:11)!

6. Reformation Theology

The early teaching of the reformists can be acquired from Luther's Heidelberg Disputations, 1518, and is summarised in 'Theologian of the Cross'. This was the foundation followed by Tyndale's New Testament, 1534 and Calvin's Institutes of Christian Religion, 1536. These major contributions were dependent upon Scripture and to a lesser extent tradition; the former being unchanging, but the latter often considered disputable. Here are some of the salient points of Reformation Theology expressed by Luther in his role as a Theologian of the Cross, stressing the following paradoxes.

The Doctrine of the power of sin, which causes total depravity. Deadly sins seduce men and women into trusting in them and their way of commitment. We are totally incapable of resisting temptation by our own free will. It is human nature to turn a blind eye to evilness and only acknowledge good deeds. We are offended, when our best works are judged by God to be deadly sins, forgetting that all our righteous acts are as filthy rags in his most holy sight (Isa. 64:6).

The Doctrine of justification in faith alone is based on the belief in the complete pardoning from all sin, which is only gained through faith in the Lord Jesus Christ and his atoning sacrifice on the Cross of Golgotha. Such total belief is given to every believer as a gift of God. Justification by faith is never gained by being good, as good works are the product and not the cause of faith.

Only a personal union with Christ regenerates a believer into a new life of good works. When all our human efforts have been exhausted and we have been reduced to nothing, the one who creates out of nothing does his proper work.

Only the righteousness of God can make a believer more righteous, through the hidden work of the Holy Spirit. We are personally in our Father's hands, as was Jesus of Nazareth during his worldly mission.

N.B. This Pauline concept of God's grace was completely inconsistent with the doctrine of the Roman Church, which continued to believe in Purgatory and praying for those afflicted in this spiritual afterlife. Such belief discredits the total efficacy of the Cross of Christ.

Scripture (Lt. *Scriptura* or writing)

The first and greatest priority of the reformers was the establishment of an accurate translation of the Word of God, which was to be made available to all believers in their own tongue! The doctrine of its infallibility and authority was dependent upon it being recognised as the Word of God, not only in its broad instruction to believers, but also in every word (Rev.22:18-19); as in the Hebrew Scroll, every 'jot and tittle' is truth and has meaning! The Bible (Gr. *Biblia* or book) contains both the Old and New Testaments from the same authorship, as all Scripture is God's witness of himself and his wish for mankind to worship him!

It is God's rightful authority as our Creator to declare that his word must be believed and obeyed. His divine words are canonical (Gr. rule or measure) being written by the prophets and the apostles under God's eternal authority. Their intent is to reveal God's creation, as conveyed by the Holy Spirit. It has been previously noted, both Testaments originate from the same source and they authenticate the same divine truth.

The Triune God

God's unity, eternity and self-existence were expressed when he declared to Moses,

> *"I AM THAT I AM."*
>
> **(Ex. 3:14 K.J.V.)**

The heavenly Father has revealed his personality and immortality in and through the power of Jesus Christ, who possesses his heavenly Father's sovereignty or glory, mercy and peace, moral attributes and justice. There is no greater source of God's revelation than that personified in Jesus Christ, who is our prophet priest and king. The Son willed his birth and his life in this world, personally, and also his death upon the cross. He suffered for the salvation of all believers given to him by his Father (Jn. 6:37–40).

The Holy Spirit is a gift from God, who represents the holy presence of Christ within all believers' hearts and reveals the truth of God's word as recorded in Scripture.

The Doctrine of the Cross

Luther described the Old Testament as 'cruciful', especially in reference to Psalms 22 and 69, and also Isaiah 53; whereas the New Testament contains the detailed story of the cross. Its implications are summed up in the following words of St. Paul,

> **"I have been crucified with Christ and no longer live, but Christ lives in me. The life I live in the body, I live by faith in the Son of God, who loved me and gave himself for me."**
>
> **(Gal. 2:20).**

The Cross must never be separated from the Resurrection; whereas the former signifies death, the latter is essential for a new life in Christ to begin and blossom. We can only die with him and await God's answer in him! Therefore the word of the Cross crucifies the old body, in anticipation of the resurrection of the new; but for a resurrection to happen there must first be a death. Luther looked at all things through suffering and the Cross, believing it to be certainly true that through Christ's passion God was entering into our suffering and death! The Cross makes those who believe part of its story; the Cross alone is our theology!

The Resurrection

The Old Testament culminates in the Cross and resurrection, the Cross being the key to its understanding and the unlocking of the entire biblical story. The word of the Cross inevitably kills, but it also makes alive. It crucifies the Old Covenant in anticipation of the resurrection of the New Covenant. It reveals to us the way things really are, for if we die with him, shall we not also live with him?

To sum up this Pauline teaching on the subject, if the death of Christ is the first and greatest step towards the salvation of all believers, the resurrection of the living God must inevitably be the second most important step for two reasons:

1. The resurrection is proof that Jesus of Nazareth is the risen Lord Jesus Christ, Son of God!
2. The resurrection of the Lord Jesus Christ led to his glorification and the promised advent of the Holy Spirit with his blessing upon the early church (Jn. 7:38-39).

7. The English Reformation

The Protestant movement (1540–1553) was inspired in England by the early efforts of John Wycliffe (Wyclif) in the 14th century (1330–84). This religious reformer was a man of the people. He translated Jerome's Latin Bible into English, as he believed that everyone had the right to hear or read the Bible in their own language. The Roman Church opposed his efforts, feeling it their duty to retain their Catholic Latin rites and deny the common people direct access to translations of the Scriptural truth.

John Wycliffe was also opposed to the abuse of the Church's traditional indulgences. These included the remission or absolution of temporal punishment, involving confession and penances as part of the sale of indulgences. None of these practices had Scriptural authority. He encouraged his followers by translating Jerome's Vulgate Bible into English. This also provided inspiration for William Tyndale to complete his own translation of the New Testament two hundred years later in 1525. Tyndale was also attracted by the work of Erasmus and Luther, which led him to travel to Wittenberg and later to Worms. In 1536, his New Testament was printed there and 50,000 copies were smuggled into England for distribution.

The Protestants gained protection from King Henry's quarrel with the Roman Church under the guidance of Hugh Latimer and Cranmer, which continued through the short reign of King Edward. In 1553, however, Mary came to the throne and submitted herself to the Church of Rome. During the last three and a half years of her reign, the Protestant Churches were purged and replaced by dignitaries of the Church of Rome. They set aside King Henry's New English Bible and Prayer Book and reintroduced Mass and images of their saints into the Churches. During this period of severe and bitter oppression, hundreds of Protestants were convicted of heresy and perished at the stake. They included such prominent leaders as Latimer, Tyndale, Frith, Ridley, Barnes, Rogers, Bradford and Cranmer. Many others escaped Queen Mary's purge by fleeing to the Continent. John Knox and other Protestants joined Calvin in Geneva, where they helped William Whittingham prepare a new translation of the Scripture called the Geneva Bible. This contained much of Tyndale's translations and was published in English in 1560. It became internationally popular because of its high standard of Reformation scholarship.

The persecution by Mary and the Roman church caused a revolt by many of her subjects and threatened a general uprising against her rule. Following her death in 1558, Elizabeth's accession was welcomed enthusiastically, as it heralded the return of Protestantism to the country! Her rule continued until 1603, when King James and a Puritan England succeeded her uncompromising reign!

8. Puritan England (1583–1685)

After the revolt and separation from the Roman Catholic Church, England suddenly became a nation of one book. This was the Geneva Bible that was set up in the churches throughout the country by the previous command of Queen Elizabeth.

The Bible became recognised as the noblest example of the English language, exerting an influence over everyday speech. The queen and her ministers tried to dampen down the overwhelming response, but they could not control the great itinerant preachers that revealed God's truth and grace towards repentant people.

The Gospel also provided an important stimulus for compassion in the social and educational services throughout the country. The whole temper of the nation was changed by the new conception of life from both moral and spiritual values. Yet it had become apparent that Elizabeth harboured a religious indifference and moderation towards the church, which suffered to some extent from the stubborn ruling of the monarch.

When the queen died in 1603, James I came to the throne. At that time the Puritan influence was high and its leaders tried to purge the Church of all the remnants of popery. In 1604 the king arranged a conference of church dignitaries to discuss the proposal for a new translation of the Bible. He stressed a preference for a revision of the unpopular Bishop's Bible, rather than the Geneva Bible that his predecessor had set up in the churches. William Perkins was made responsible for organising the revision, but to hasten their huge task it was decided to include much of the content of the superior Geneva script that was largely made up of Tyndale's original translations. The authorised version of the King James Bible was published in 1611 and it gradually replaced the older Bibles throughout England. Its popularity has continued due to its high standard of prose and clarity that makes it easier to memorise. The king also upheld the use of the Common Prayer Book, which was revised to provide a new liturgy for the church. In the old pre-Reformation Prayer Book the 'Publick Liturgy' was mainly written in Latin, which could not be understood by the majority of the laity. It consisted of Scriptural material, but also included antiphons and devotional material from many sources. These fictitious details concerning Rites and Ceremonies were embellished by fanciful facts about the Lives of Saints.

In the Revised Book of Common Prayer the Christian liturgy, or system of Divine Service in the churches, contained an Order of Prayer based on New Testament readings. They were divided into two parts, namely the 'Gospel' (Evangelistarium) and the 'Apostle' (Apostolos) each being accepted as emanating from apostolic instruction. The first part included the three Synoptic Gospels, in which were recorded the events and sayings from the life of Jesus. John's Gospel was also included, being similar to the Synoptic Gospels in much of its witness, but it also contained the inscribed teachings of the risen Lord. Although written in the post-Pentecostal period, it retrospectively revealed the divinity of the Logos in its prologue. The 'Apostle' was made up of the remaining books in the New Testament, including Acts, the Epistles and Revelation. They contained the theological instructions of the risen Lord, which were revealed by the Holy Spirit to the Apostles in order to complement the doctrine in the Gospels. Therefore the greater part of the new Bible was read over once a year, including the Old and New Testaments in addition to Morning and Evening Prayers! The continuity of Scriptural readings was maintained, at the expense of Anthems, Responses and Invitatories.

The reading of Scripture in the English tongue throughout the Churches was a new adventure, which fell on the ears of a previously 'starved' population that were 'rabid' for the food of God. It was received as manna from heaven (Jn. 6:32–33)! The people flocked to hear the audibly spoken Word of God, as recorded in both Old and New Testaments. For the ordinary people, this was a new source of enlightenment and cleansing from a previously darkened world (Jn. 15:3). Such readings have become a traditional rite in Church liturgy and remain even today.

The reign of Charles I was a troublesome period for the Church, due to the conflict between the Royalist followers and the Protestant Parliament. This culminated in a civil war and eventually the execution of the king in 1649. Subsequently, Cromwell's Protectorate became a triumph for a political Puritism that allowed free Protestant worship. In 1643 some of the greatest contemporary Puritan leaders of the churches in England, Scotland and Ireland were brought together to form the Westminster assembly. Their aim was to produce a Confession to unite all three churches. They drew up a Confession of faith and also the Larger and Smaller Catechisms published in 1646. The former was made up of mainly Puritan theology; whereas the latter contained declarations of faith, including Old and New Testament texts. They were to be memorised by every participant of the liturgy. These documents were recognised even by their critics to have had a great spiritual influence over all the liturgical and Protestant churches in the four home countries, and even further afield. Some remnants of these declarations are included in the present day editions of the Book of Common Prayer and more recent instructions in the services and prayers for the Church of England.

During the reign of Charles II, many Puritans were driven out of their liturgical churches, because they dissented from the compulsory use of the Common Prayer Book. The dissenters included a lay preacher named John Bunyan, who later became recognised as one of the more influential Puritan leaders. His books remain some of the most popular in English Christian literature, especially the one entitled Pilgrim's Progress and published in 1678.

John Owen and Matthew Henry were also leading

Puritans. Yet some considered the Scottish Covenanters to be the last of the Puritans, because in 1660–88 they resisted the claims of both kings (Charles II and James II) to being the head of their Church. But by the beginning of the eighteenth century, Puritanism had become spiritually dormant throughout the established Church.

Yet the Calvinistic insistence on the use of the Bible readings alone inhibited the development of hymn writing and singing in England until the 18th century evangelical revival.

In the wilderness of Christian belief, the embers of faith still smouldered and were ready to burst into flames when fanned and revived by the Holy Spirit. Previous to the great awakening in North America, instigated by the preaching of Jonathan Edwards in 1735–40, revival came to this country in 1729 breaking out at first in the University of Oxford. A group of young academic visionaries joined to form an evangelical society called the 'Holy Club' by their scoffers. They met regularly for Bible Studies and hymn singing. At other times they offered their services to the poor and needy. This eventually earned them another name, that of 'Methodism'. The leaders of the Society were two brothers named John and Charles Wesley and a friend called George Whitefield, all three becoming responsible for the Methodist Movement. They believed that God responded, by the outpouring of the Holy Spirit, to continuing prayers of thankfulness following repentance (1 Thes. 5:16–18). These three great reformers helped to shape a revival of the Word of God throughout the English-speaking world during the latter part of the eighteenth century. Their influence was within and without the established Church, the former followers becoming known as evangelicals, while the latter became the non-conforming evangelical denominations. Both of these movements remain in the vanguard of Christian evangelism in the modern world crusade.

9. Revival

To the dwindling number of people able to recall Dr. Martyn Lloyd-Jones' ministry and expository preaching, he was believed to be the last of the Puritans. The memory of his zeal and passion for the exposition of Scripture will live forever in their minds. He believed that revival could break out in his congregation, wherever he was declaring the indescribable Word of God. At his 'surgery' held following every Sunday evening service, there was an open door to any member of the congregation with a personal problem. Yet he hastened to tell them that he was powerless to change their lives, but that God could do anything and was often persuaded by prayer! He believed revival was due to the same divine power that brings about the conversion of every believer, when extended to many at the same time. It is the same vital awareness, always present wherever there is true Christian belief, which in the days of revival abounds and overflows. The same Holy Spirit known to every single believer is then 'outpoured' upon a multitude (Dr. M. Lloyd-Jones).

The Doctor believed that none had the power to induce one single true conversion, as only God can perform miracles! 'The same sovereign and supernatural power, which is essential to the saving of one individual is equally indispensable in the case of the revival conversion of many. Yet men and women, singly or in multitudes, are not brought to faith without first hearing the Word of God and understanding the Gospel of Christ!

Therefore revival is essentially a corporate occurrence, an infectious enlivening of a number of persons by the Holy Spirit, not in isolation but together! There are instances of both multiple and single conversions in Scripture. When Peter addressed the men of Israel with the Gospel of the crucifixion of Jesus Christ, about three thousand repented and were baptised, being added to their number in the early Christian Church that day! (Ac. 2:38–41)! And later, when Philip had expounded the book of Isaiah (Ch. 53:7–8) and the good news about Jesus to the Ethiopian eunuch, instant conversion occurred, as witnessed by the response, "What doth hinder me to be baptized?" (Ac. 8:36. K.J.V.).On each occasion, Scripture records that the Holy Spirit was instrumental in conveying God's saving grace to those who repented and believed in the Word of God!

10. Modern Christian Worship

Following Revival, corporate worship abounded in both liturgical and non-liturgical churches along similar converging ecumenical patterns, including music and the singing of hymns. It proved attractive to all believers in the various denominations with few exceptions. The centrality of Scriptural truth was recognised by all, both in the reading and exposition. The latter was mainly in sermon form, but also by the repetition of the Creed and other articles of faith. Corporate prayer and the partaking of Holy Communion became highlights of the services.

Subsequently, Holy Communion (the fellowship of believers) has become recognised to be the highest form of continuous expression of Christian belief, without any hint of transubstantiation! The liturgical churches use settled forms of corporate worship, founded on theology. They are expressed in collective texts, spoken in the traditional form conforming to historical devotional practice. Such liturgical theology interprets the teachings of Scripture in Old and New Testaments.

The Doxologies express the beliefs and praises in the worship of the Triune God. They are the spiritual glorification of God, which has been described as, 'the language of the heart' expressing belief in devotional praise. Therefore Christian liturgy is founded upon the revelation of Scriptural truth containing the following biblical principles, previously listed under Reformation Theology.

Justification by faith

In God's plan of salvation, all human effort to gain redemption in the sight of their Creator-God is doomed to failure because believers' righteousness depends not on merit earned by men and women, but on God's saving grace in Jesus Christ. Luther's great conclusion has become the foundation of Protestant belief and Christian worship, proclaiming justification "through obedience that comes from faith" (Ro. 1:5, 6:5–7). It remains the main difference between the two faiths, the Roman Catholic instruction on justification being that it is gained by personal effort and sacrifice, rather than a gift of grace given to all believers from their heavenly Father through his only begotten Son (Eph. 2:8–10).

Scripture and preaching

The Reformed Denominations have always believed in the infallibility and authority of the Word of God in all matters of doctrine. Although there remains great respect for the traditional practices of the church, the majority believe them to be subservient to the true word of the Gospel of Christ (Col. 1:5). The Holy Spirit employs the truth of the Gospel to bring about the conversion of all believers, and he does so supremely by the agency of preaching the Word of God in the churches of all denominations. Therefore preaching with such assurance is gained through the power of the Holy Spirit within the hearts of men and women. Such a rewarding service is gained by preaching the truth of God, which is mainly the product of the power of Scripture rather than intellect. This witness is owned by God to be the true Gospel!

Expository preaching expresses the mystery of God and his love in a simple and lucid manner. It follows the same pattern practised by Jesus of Nazareth. As has been said, men and women are never brought to faith without first hearing the Word of God, either singly or in multitudes.

St. Paul said,

> **"Yet when I preach the gospel, I cannot boast, for I am compelled to preach. Woe to me if I do not preach the gospel."**
>
> **(1 Cor. 9:16)**

C.H. Spurgeon declared in 1883,

> *"In the beginning the preacher's business is not to convert men, but the very reverse! It is idle to attempt to heal those who are not wounded, to attempt to clothe those who have never been stripped, and to make those rich who have never realised their poverty!*

Evangelical sermons proclaim the Gospel and the power of God, as revealed by the Holy Spirit. Jesus said of the Counsellor,

"He will prove the world to be in the wrong about sin and righteousness and judgement."
(Jn. 16:8)

The Holy Spirit will convince us of our guilt! This is referred to as the awakening of spiritual concern, which involves being alerted to the convicting powers of sin (Jn. 8:46. K.J.V.). Unless we realise our deep and desperate need of the love of God, it is of no value to us and will make no difference to our lives.

"It is made perfectly clear in the pages of the New Testament that no man can be saved, until at some time or another he has felt desperate about himself."
(Dr.M.Lloyd-.Jones.)

It is of deep regret that modern religious authority is discreetly covering over the dangers of satanic powers in this evil world and even denying the existence of the 'prince of this world', the 'prince of darkness' (Jn. 16:11; 2 Cor. 11:14; Col. 1:13).

Baptism

The Protestant Reformers rejected the Roman Catholic interpretation of all seven sacraments, including those concerned with the traditional rites of confirmation, matrimony, penance, unction and ordination; but they retained in different forms those of baptism and communion, as they were the only two sacraments recorded in the Gospels. Both rites were ordered by the explicit commands of Jesus of Nazareth, as each reflected the Covenantal instruction of the Old Testament concerning circumcision and the Passover respectively.

As has been said before, the Biblical theology of the sacramental rite of baptism had its deep roots in the Old Covenant, being mentioned in Scripture as part of ceremonial washing of the priests on the Day of Atonement. It was a purification rite before entry into the sanctuary of the LORD. Washing with pure water was also used with ritual circumcision in the initiation of the Gentiles into Judaism. Then in the New Testament, John the Baptist continued the practice of total immersion, as a conversion rite into the Christian faith (Jn. 1:26).

Today the Protestant churches practise baptism, as a confession of faith either by sprinkling or immersion. It is used in infant baptism to enrol a newborn into the Christian Church, or alternatively as an adult confession of faith into the fellowship of the church; the former being an introduction into the kingdom of God and the latter recognition of regeneration and new birth in which water signifies the Holy Spirit. Both forms of baptism are ritual, in recognition of the baptism of Jesus in the river Jordan (Mt. 3:15). The sanctification of water represents the mystical washing away of sin (Jn. 3:5–8).

Spiritual Baptism

Yet John declared that Jesus would baptise with the Holy Spirit, testifying that this gift of purification would supersede his baptism of water (Jn. 1:32–34; Ac. 1:5;

1 Cor. 12:13). Only Christ the Son of God possesses the divine power to forgive a sinner through the authority bestowed upon him by his heavenly Father. This miraculous achievement is performed through the Holy Spirit on those chosen and called by God. It follows the confession of their sinful estate and repentance through the atoning sacrifice of their Saviour and Redeemer.

Scripture refers to Spiritual baptism being God's gift of the Spirit of Christ, to dwell in the hearts of all believers from the moment of their conversion (Ro. 8:9; Gal. 3:2). Subsequently the Holy Spirit continues to unite the believer to Christ through the process of sanctification.

During the Christian pilgrimage in this world, the Holy Spirit continuously regenerates a believer's heart and soul, testifying to his or her adoption by Christ. He regenerates and illuminates the word of God and provides gifts of service and sustains our prayers.

Yet many believe that Spiritual Baptism also refers to a special gift from God to mature Christians, as a second blessing. In such instances it is an indescribable gift given as a reward for total dedication to Christ, given as a seal or guarantee of eternal life in fellowship with the heavenly Father and Son (Jn. 17:3; 1 Jn. 1:3). It is a final goal offered to all believers who dedicate themselves as living sacrifices to God's service (Ro. 12:1–2) and is identified in the recipients by a saintly visible illumination, or revival of the soul with the peace and righteousness of God's very presence and rule (Php. 3:12).

This form of spiritual baptism may affect a gathering of believers, as befell the disciples on the Day of Pentecost (Acts 2). They had already been converted and made clean through the words spoken to them by Jesus (Jn. 15:3) and had received the Holy Spirit breathed on them by the risen Lord (Jn. 20:22). Later they were instructed to remain in Jerusalem and wait for the gift the heavenly Father had promised, baptism with the Holy Spirit (Acts 1:4–5). When this happened, they were filled with the Holy Spirit and enabled to speak in other tongues (Acts 2:1–4).

There are two personal signs of this maturity, the first being a constant awareness of one's sin in the sight of God (Isa. 64:6), producing a profound and saintly humility in the presence of fellow believers. This profound humility is accompanied by a daily thirst and hunger for the righteousness of Jesus Christ, only alleviated by Scripture reading and prayer. Such holiness is revealed in personal and even in public prayers.

The Lord's Supper (Eucharist)

This is a religious rite that dates back to the early Christian Church, being included in the 'Didache', or the 'Teaching of the Twelve Apostles'. It originated in one of the three Great Feasts of the Jews, Passover (*Pesah Heb.).*This is a feast held by the Jews before the 'Week of Unleavened Bread', called Haggadah, which is held in remembrance of the Exodus or great escape from Egyptian Captivity (Ex. 12:1–11). The Passover Lamb had to be sacrificed for this Love Feast, *'Agape'*, and food was given to the poor. The brother of Jesus mentioned this briefly in the New Testament (Jude 12).

On the night that he was betrayed, Jesus used the occasion to prophesy the manner of his impending execution. He commanded his disciples that they repeat the institution in continual remembrance of his atoning sacrifice (Mt. 26:26–29; Mk. 14:22–25; Lk. 22:17–20). The Anglican Church has its own order of the Administration of the Lord's Supper, whereas the Protestant Denominations use the words of St. Paul for the Communion (1 Cor. 11:23–29).

Therefore the majority of modern Christian churches practise repeatedly the Lord's Supper, as a Fellowship of Believers. Yet they reject the doctrine of transubstantiation of the Eucharist!

The Clergy

The confinement of religious authority to appointed clergy caused discontent in many of the lay population. It gained even less support once Scripture was made available to all. Also the doctrine of the priesthood of all believers is Scriptural in authority (1 Pe. 2:9–10) and has gained universal agreement. It radically changed the layman's attitude towards ordained priests and ministers of the churches. Whereas the majority of the general public continue to hold them in high esteem, only the minority of modern believers accept their role as sole mediators in their relation to the Triune God, with regard to confession and absolution of sins.

Church and State

The Protestants have never sought political power on the advice of their Lord and Saviour (Mt. 22:21) but have always prayed for government guidance in the fulfilment of God's will both in spiritual realms and worldly politics. A few radical reformers have sought to separate their church from state control, but the majority are law abiding in everyday worldly matters.

Thus corporate worship is entirely dependent upon the modern theological understanding of Scripture, which provides a concept based on acceptable spoken texts in their devotional forms of worship practised in our churches and houses of prayer. This includes systems of public devotion in both liturgical and non-liturgical forms. It has evolved from the historic practice of the interpretation of biblical truth. This constitutes a modern approach to liturgical theology. It must necessarily reflect one's personal beliefs that are reinforced by communal worship with believers of similar faith.

11. Conclusions

There is a considerable overlap in the liturgy of the various denominations in modern forms of worship, which minimises the opportunity for dissent. This is understandable, as all ecumenical Christian belief is founded upon the centrality of the Triune God, Father, Son and Holy Spirit, and the personal knowledge of Scripture. Such faith enlightens our bodies and souls and encourages all forms of worship in spirit and in truth!

This modern attitude arose following the Reformation and was based on the instructions given by the overpowering authority of its founders, including Luther, Calvin and Tyndale who were the leaders of the dissenters from Roman Catholicism. They firmly believed in their five biblical principles, which remain upheld by all the various Protestant denominations, apart from the Roman Catholic Church.

In 1517 Luther nailed his Ninety-Five Theses to the door of the Castle Church in Wittenberg objecting to the sale of indulgences in the Roman Catholic Church. One wonders how many theses would be nailed upon the door of our modern Christian Churches throughout the country, if he returned today.

1. Would he be critical of the lack of faith in the authority and infallibility of the Word of God that has been allowed to pervade the Church and even the law of Parliament? This appears to have led to the prosecution of Christians who stand up for the principles of their Christian faith, where human rights are being upheld in our courts against the Law of God and the righteousness of Christ!
2. Another criticism might be aimed at the freedom to worship religions that preach against Jewish and Christian faiths; and the building of edifices to glorify such faiths in an attempt to overshadow the established belief that supports the very infrastructure of British heritage!
3. Would he express abhorrence against the acceptance of homosexuality, as being a normal feature of human affection, rather than a sinful practice in the eyes of God and an offence to human nature? Such criticism might also include the imposition of 'same-sex marriages' over and above normal human behaviour.
4. There would also be criticism of the proposed right to take one's own life, as above the sanctity of all human life in the sight of God (Ps. 139:16) and an impending threat to medical practitioners who refuse to administer lethal doses of drugs to their patients at their request!

It seems apparent that there is only a remnant of people in our country who fear the Lord and beware his wrath (Ps. 90:11–12, Ac. 10:35). Is it not time to pray for revival, to overcome the growing prevalence of apathy among the younger generation? It will only come if the words of Luther are recalled and upheld in our personal and corporate worship,

"I simply taught, preached and wrote God's Word:
I did nothing – the Word of God did it all."

CHAPTER 9

GOD'S REGULATIONS OF WORSHIP

1. Introduction

God has spoken on two occasions to the house of Israel to reveal his will concerning the divine relationship between him and his chosen people. Each time his words have been in the form of a holy obligation with a promise for those who obey. His two divine commands have been linked to a regulation of worship for all who fear his most holy name (Heb. 6:13–15; 8:10–13).

The first command was included in the Old Covenant between the LORD and the Israelites.

"Consecrate yourselves and be holy, because I am the LORD your God."

(Lev. 20:7)

Since the first regulation of worship was given to Moses and Aaron, (*see* pages 36–38) the command to be holy and the promise to be their God remained unchanged from the earliest days of Hebrew faith. Malachi prophesied the conclusion of the Mosaic revelation, which was followed by 400 years of silence before the advent of the Christian Gospel.

The second command was included in a New Covenant of grace and redemption between the heavenly Father and his creation. It was proclaimed through his Son,

Jesus Christ, who was the ratifying sacrifice (Mk. 14:24; Heb. 9:14).Jesus believed the greatest commandment was,

"Love the Lord your God with all your heart and with all your soul and with all your mind."
(Mt. 22:37, *see* ***Dt. 6:4*****)**

Whereas, the second was likened to it;

"Love your neighbour as yourself."
(*Lev. 19:18*; Mt. 22:39; Mk. 12:30-31; Jn. 13: 34-35)

To these he added two new precepts, or teachings:

"Remain in me, as I also remain in you."
"Love each other, as I have loved you."
(Jn.15:4,12,)

The only true Son of God repeated these commandments and added his precepts to emphasise the importance of his Father's divine love (Jn. 5:20; 1 Cor. 13:13).They were invariably linked to the promise that all who obey will become citizens of his eternal kingdom, on earth and in heaven.

In the gospel of the New Testament, Jesus heralded the New Covenant of Love (*agape*) between God and mankind! It contains the good news from the same divine source, as revealed in the Old Testament. This explains why the two revelations remain in complete harmony with each other from their very beginning. Each regulation included the same Holy Law and Promise, there being no inconsistencies between their divine content (Mt. 5:17–19). Retrospectively, the former Mosaic regulation of worship concerning the Israelite approach to the most holy presence of God was complex and obscure, compared to the clarity of Christ's latter regulation that was to come.

The former and latter regulations of worship were both copies of the pattern of the eternal and unchanging 'ordinances (or ministry) of divine worship', which continues in the heavenly Sanctuary (Heb. 8:5,9:1). Although the New Covenant made the first one obsolete (Heb. 8:13) it must always be remembered that both covenants and regulations emanated from the same Divine authority. As Jesus said,

> **"The kingdom of heaven is like the owner of a house who brings out of his storeroom, new treasures as well as old."**
>
> **(Mt. 13:52)**

This doctrine was the foundation of Augustine's declaration, quoted at the beginning of this monograph –

> *'The New Testament is latent, or hidden in the Old Testament*
> *and the Old Testament is patent, or made manifest in the New Testament.'*

Jesus is the mediator of the New Covenant. He spans the gulf between the most holy presence of his heavenly Father and the worship of all believers redeemed by his atoning sacrifice. He reveals the faithfulness and unfailing love of God offered to them through grace alone. In addition, the Holy Spirit instructs all repentant believers on how to acknowledge and respond to this divine love in their worship. Therefore, to fulfil these two commands concerning God's regulation of worship, it is helpful for all Christians to study and compare the Scriptural instructions of worship under the Old and New Covenants respectively, as found in the two Testaments. This knowledge will encourage all believers to worship truthfully and responsively through the three Persons of the Holy Trinity. The Sanctuary of the eternal Tabernacle prevails in the celestial paradise (Heb. 8:2), where the elders, prophets, apostles, martyrs and saints join with the angels in observing and fulfilling its ministry or 'ordinances of divine worship'.

2. God's Former Regulation of Worship

The Israelites were invited by the Spirit of God to attend the earthly tabernacle made by human hands. They were instructed never to come empty-handed, but to bring their offerings and sacrifices to the gate of the court. After confessing their sins, the worshippers imputed their transgressions by 'the placing of hands' on the sacrifice, before rendering the offering to the priest. Following the absolution of their sins, they were allowed entry into the outer court. They washed their hands and feet in the Laver or Basin, symbolising their cleansing by the Spirit of God. After the offerings had been sacrificed by the shedding of blood, the priest then presented the flesh as burnt offerings on the altar to produce an aroma pleasing to God! Ultimately the worshippers gained a remote approach into God's most holy presence through the mediation of the sanctified High Priest.

Copies of the plan of the celestial Tabernacle with the eternal and unchanging 'ordinances of divine worship' had been given to Moses to instruct the Israelites in their approach to the holy dwelling place (2 Ch. 6:21; 30:27); so by God's grace they might gain representation in his most holy presence, albeit through a mediator. The Holy Spirit revealed to them this three-step act or pattern of worship imposed by the layout of the plan of the earthly tabernacle. It encouraged them to climb the ladder of faith from their sinful estate, through a process of sanctification. This was to be followed by representation through mediation, fulfilling the conveyance of their devotions into the most holy presence of God.

Such a complex 'former regulation of worship' was performed annually in the rituals of *Yom Kippur* (The Day of Atonement, *see* Lev. 16:1–34). In comparison with that to come, it was a dim reflection of the eternal 'ordinances of divine worship' continuing in the true Tabernacle set up by the Lord (Heb. 8:1–6)! Yet the Holy Spirit succeeded in revealing to them this '*economy of worship*' based on copies of the 'ordinances of divine worship', which include the three steps previously recorded (Chapter 2, page 37–8). The former regulation revealed God's provisional guidance on worship, which was meant to last up to the time of the Second Covenant. It was promised that the latter would not only provide a more perfect fulfilment, but also clarity of access.

3. God's Latter Regulation of Worship

Since God is unchanging, his commands and laws are the same today compared to those recorded in the Old Testament (Ex. 20:1–17). Nothing has altered in the relationship between his holy estate and his sinful creation, in that they remain separated by an impassable gulf to preserve God's sanctity. The same relationship applies to all believers, even today, because of that remnant of inherited and acquired sin found in their hearts. During the early days of his life in this world, Jesus attended the synagogues and temples, accepting the Old Covenant and its former regulation of worship. Yet during his ministry, his disciples were instructed in new precepts and principles of worship, as a means of enlightenment compared to the complexity of the former regulation.

This indicates that it is still incumbent upon all Christians to fulfil these regulations of worship to the Triune God; for it must be their greatest hope to be chosen to continue this pattern of worship eternally, within the divine ordinances of the paradisiacal kingdom of heaven! So it is expedient to recall the order of the former Mosaic-Levitical plan in our worship in accordance with the same pattern observed in paradise, under the guidance of the Holy Spirit (*see* page 7).

Concerning the better things that God has provided for us, as compared to the blessings revealed in the first covenant and all the additional blessings of the second covenant we have, above everything declared, a new High Priest! He is superior to all predecessors and his appointment is eternal!

As author of the eternal and unchanging ordinances of divine worship observed in the heavenly Tabernacle of the paradisiacal kingdom, Jesus had no apparent wish other than to preserve the three-step pattern reflected in the Old Covenant (Mt. 5:17–19).By providing a direct spiritual access of worship into the most holy presence of our heavenly Father, Jesus Christ reveals his superiority to the angels who were God's messengers to the prophets and people under the Old Covenant. Through Christ's mediation, we draw nearer to God in spirit, as he responds to us in our daily worship. Christ has facilitated this new spiritual approach through his body, making straight the way for the Lord and his followers (Isa. 40:3; Jn. 1:23). Through the advocacy of the Holy Spirit, believers might enter spiritually into Christ's very presence. He cleanses and covers believers with robes of humility and righteousness, making them fit to approach the Most Holy Place in the heavenly Tabernacle and commune with the heavenly Father through his mediation (Isa. 61:10; Mt. 22:11; Rev. 19:7–8).

The Lord Jesus Christ has provided himself, as a perfect sacrifice for the redemption and atonement of those who love him. This blessing has been purchased through his precious blood by giving his life for their salvation! As blood-bought believers, our heavenly Father forgives our wickedness and will remember our sins no more (Jer. 31:34; Heb. 10:17). Therefore a new approach and a new sacrifice, to which is added a new promise of the advent of a Paraclete or Counsellor, being his Holy Spirit who has purchased an eternal life in the most holy presence of the heavenly Father. These promises were given to those who believe in the saving power of God's Son, our Saviour.

Therefore each member of the Holy Trinity plays a vital role in our spiritual approach to God's holy presence in his paradisiacal kingdom. The redeeming power of his atoning sacrifice won our Saviour the divine right to become his Father's chosen mediator, spanning the gulf between God's most holy estate and his sinful people. This great act of forgiving grace provides every Christian with the awesome privilege of a spiritual entry into the most holy presence of the heavenly Father in the paradisiacal Sanctuary, which is the very essence and centrality of true worship.

To benefit from this great act of salvation, it is essential for every believer to accept that all forms of prayer include this approach in spirit and truth through each member of the Trinity (Jn. 4:23–24). This is the unfailing pathway along which a Christian is able to express a spiritual response to the faithful love of the heavenly Father. Such a miraculous transcendence is above all human understanding. It is fulfilled by the forgiving grace of the Lord Jesus and his Holy Spirit who is Christ's spiritual presence within their hearts (Ex. 33:14; Dt. 30:11–14; Ro. 8:9; Eph. 3:16–17). This form of prayer is the most effective channel of true worship, during which the participant seeks an entry into God's most holy presence in the heavenly Sanctuary.

But when asked by his disciples on how to pray, Jesus provided an additional enlightenment on this form of worship. He simply pronounced three basic principles, embracing six petitions, governing the relationship between the holiness of his heavenly Father and all sinful and humble creatures. These principles were to be accepted in their original order providing the foundation for the three-step pattern of the latter regulation in divine worship. The petitions were also given in a priority listing, the first three being divine and the last three personal, as found in,

4. "The Lord's Prayer"

(Mt. 6:9-13; Lk. 11:2-4)

The essence of true prayer is proclaimed in the opening words,

"Our Father, in heaven!"

These introductory words establish the first and most important principle that has since been entitled, 'Recognition and Appeal'. The former includes recognition of the worshipper's lowly estate and the supreme privilege given to sinners saved by grace, in their approach to such an awesome, holy and righteous heavenly Father. The writer of Ecclesiastes reminded his readers of this awesome notion,

"God is in heaven and you are on earth."
(Ecc. 5:2)

It has been said repeatedly that there is an impenetrable gulf between the most holy presence of God and all people including believers. Recognition of our heavenly Father's supreme concession of a spiritual entry into his most holy presence should always persuade every worshipper to pause and try to realise what they are hoping to fulfil! This made Jacob more than afraid, almost petrified, for he called out, "How awesome is the place! This is none other than the house of God; this is the gate of heaven" (Ge. 28:17). Later God commanded Moses and Joshua, "Do not come any closer; take off your sandals, for the place where you are standing is holy ground" (Ex. 3:5). The ground was made holy, due to the presence of the LORD (Jos. 5:15).

This recognition clarifies the need for an appeal, or an invocation, to a higher advocate for assistance in fulfilling this communion in the spiritual worship of God. We find ourselves dependent upon the advocacy of the Holy Spirit and the mediation of our Lord Jesus Christ in order to span this barrier. One has to be accepted into the family of God to receive the Spirit of adoption, before repeating the words, "Abba, Father." with reverence and fear (Gal. 4:6). For to be enabled to truthfully say these opening words, from the bottom of your heart, means you have qualified for this great honour by showing the reverential awe of a true believer! Therefore, one should never rush into the presence of God, but start one's prayer by remembering past sins and then pleading forgiveness before attempting to worship him!

The second principle has been entitled, 'Adoration', an act of worship expressing our profound deep love to our Saviour and heavenly Father. It embraces the first three divine petitions,

"Hallowed be your name; your kingdom come;
your will be done,
on earth as it is in heaven."

These are all expressions of God's glory. It has been pointed out that three is the number of persons in the Trinity, consisting of the Father, Son and Holy Spirit. This is an indication to us that our worship must be offered equally among the members of the Deity. An acknowledgment of the power and glory of the Holy Spirit, as our supreme advocate, is included in this first step of our prayer. This must lead to our worship of the Son, our saviour and mediator, who reveals the glory of God our heavenly Father. However great and pressing our personal needs may be, we must first attend to the worship of our Triune God, including their honour, power and glory. Any meagreness in our concern over God's glory reflects a lack of respect for his goodness, kindness and providence. In his High Priestly prayer, Jesus' first concern was his Father's glory that he had striven to reveal to men and women on earth (Jn. 17:4). Therefore the first petition involves humbling oneself in adoring the presence of our Saviour and worshipping the heavenly Father, by witnessing his most holy name against the surrounding kingdom of darkness and evil (Dr. M. Lloyd-Jones).

We should all have a consuming passion that others might come to know God and his forgiving grace. Our one great contribution should be to reflect God's glory, his faithfulness, love and forgiving grace to all around us in this darkened world! This is the reason for these first three divine petitions often being called an all-inclusive missionary prayer for evangelising everyone on God's earth. The coming of God's kingdom of heaven, in which he reigns, was the divine promise of the Old Covenant. It was fulfilled by the advent of Jesus Christ, who represented the 'kingdom of God' during his life in this world. After his death, resurrection and ascension, Christ fulfilled his ministry by sending the Holy Spirit to continue his reign in the hearts of all believers in his Church. Therefore this must be the most urgent part of our prayer, until the dawn of God's day when righteousness will dwell in a new heaven and a new earth (2 Pe. 3:12–13)!

Finally the third petition is the logical consequence arising out of the first and second petitions, when God's rule will be done on earth as it is in heaven. Only then will his glory shine over the entire universe! Unfortunately the world has not known the love of God (Jn. 17:25–26) and the majority of people consider him to be a harsh ruler. But the world would be his kingdom if everyone knew of the faithfulness, love and forgiving grace of our heavenly Father. Therefore our greatest wish is for the spread of God's kingdom, as today our greatest concern for the future is the reality of the existence of the widespread sin and wickedness in our world!

The third principle has subsequently been entitled, 'Supplication', which includes our own personal petitions or requests to the heavenly Father.

"Give us today our daily bread.
And forgive us our debts, as we also have forgiven our debtors.
And lead us not into temptation, but deliver us from all evil."

These last three petitions include our own essential needs, as they refer to our daily bread, the forgiveness of our sins and protection from temptation and evil. This embraces inclusively everything we so desperately need in our lives in this world. They include the needs of our body, soul and spirit, in priority order!

Our daily bread is an essential food for our health and our physical needs, without which we would succumb. The forgiveness of personal sins that torment our souls prevents mental stress and anguish. Finally, the protection from all evil is essential, if we hope to continue our lives eternally in the presence of the Triune God (Jn. 17:2–3).

These were the blessings poured onto the head of Adam by his Creator in the Garden of Eden, as he walked in fellowship and communion with God creating a perfect paradise. He and his dependants lost many of these privileges, as the result of his fall from God's grace. Therefore Adam's progeny (the Israelites) had to continually pray for their daily bread (manna) and for the bread for tomorrow (mahar) as their God was concerned with every detail of their lives in the desert.

***"These are the ones I look on with favour:
those who are humble and contrite in spirit,
who tremble at my word."***

(Isa. 66:2.)

It has been said that God does not give his children 'lump sums', but provides his blessings in instalments. Although he knows our every need, he enjoys listening to our faltering personal requests day in and day out throughout our lives. We are in his hands. God's love for his people accounts for the whole miracle of redemption, including the incarnation of Jesus Christ our Saviour, followed by the advent of the Holy Spirit on the day of Pentecost.

God's promises never fail, and he is not slow in keeping them (2 Pe. 3:9). But, even when Christians live in a paradisiacal life of faith, they are also liable to fall into sin. As we walk through life, our feet are likely to be soiled by sin and need washing (Jn. 13:10). It has been said, the greater the saint, the greater is his sense of personal sin, the awareness of the sins within his heart (1 Jn. 1: 8–9)! The need to forgive others reminds us of our own needs (Mt. 18:21–35).

The last petition is also a warning of the presence of the evil one, the prince of darkness who spends much of his time tempting believers, as he attempted to do to Jesus in the wilderness (Mt. 4:1–11). God never tempts his children, but he often tests those he loves! He warns us of the risk caused by the remnant of evilness within our own hearts. Therefore this final petition is a comprehensive warning to all Christians. Our supreme desire is to be able to stand in the presence of God (Lk. 1:19). Nothing must come between this communion, to know him and to love him (Dr. M. Lloyd-.Jones.).

Finally, the Lord's Prayer ends with glorious words,

"For thine is the kingdom, and the power, and the glory, for ever.
Amen."

These words constitute a doxology that is included in some of the older translations including the King James Version. It has been excluded from more recent translations, as it is not known for certain that the Lord Jesus Christ uttered these appropriate words. Yet they end this most wonderful portion of Scripture with our praise and thanksgiving for God's forgiving grace in our daily lives!

Conclusions

In these original instructions, Jesus taught his disciples the fundamental principles and petitions involved in worshipping the heavenly Father, without implying explicitly about praying in his name. But this was implicit from the very beginning, as no one can truthfully say, "Our Father in heaven" without knowing the Lord Jesus Christ and praying through his mediation. Jesus also informed his followers concerning the advent of the Holy Spirit; this Advocate had been chosen to teach his children all things, which included spiritual prayer (Jn. 14:25). He would guide them in all the Scriptural truths, which they had been incapable of receiving from Jesus before his death (Jn. 16:12–15).

Later in his ministry, Jesus gave further instructions concerning the manner in which they should pray, but these were to be obeyed once the risen Lord had left them and ascended into heaven. Then they should always ask the heavenly Father in and through his name, and they would receive anything that he himself would give if he were with them (Jn. 16:23).

Therefore the approach to true prayer under the New Covenant has been gradually unfolded, step-by-step, throughout both Testaments. By God's good grace, the previous impediment to man's access in his prayerful approach to the most holy presence of the heavenly Father has been overcome by Christ's atoning sacrifice.

"For through him we both (Jews and Gentiles) have access to the Father by one Spirit."
(Eph. 2:18)

The final outcome of Christ's gospel must embrace a form of 'latter regulation of worship' that truly reflects the eternal and unchanging pattern explicit in the 'ordinances of divine worship' observed in the heavenly Tabernacle in the paradisiacal kingdom! It has been seen that Christ's instructions on prayer provided, not so much a new pattern of worship for his disciples to follow, but more a recognition of the all-important principles in priority listing that should rule the minds of all worshippers. The Lord's Prayer has been described as a framework on which to hang the details of his principles including our recognition, adoration and supplication with our petitions. They should be embraced within the three vital steps fulfilled in the 'former regulation of worship', as clarified under the Old and New Covenants.

So let us fulfil our obligations by ascending the ladder of faith and praying through the advocacy of the Holy Spirit. He exists within our hearts and will raise us up spiritually into the heavenly realms, to enter Christ's gate with thanksgiving and into his courts with praise (Ps. 100:45; Jn. 10:9, 14:6). Then by the divine salvation and mediation of our Saviour and Redeemer, we may be granted permission to enter into the outer sanctuary of God's Tabernacle in the paradisiacal kingdom. Finally the Holy Spirit will lead our sanctified souls through the veil of Christ's body. (Heb. 10:19–20, K.J.) When clothed in the garments of his humility and righteousness, we are fully prepared for entry into the dwelling place of the most holy presence of the heavenly Father in the inner sanctuary, to present our petitions to him (Mt. 22:1–14; Lk. 14:15). As has been said before, the essence of true worship implies a spiritual entry into the very presence of God our heavenly Father (Ps. 27:4–9; 2 Ki. 17:23; 1 Th. 3:9 and 13).

The mandatory part of prayer should be an every morning grace, our daily bread, whereas the latter two voluntary parts are added whenever possible to provide the thrill and joy of communion with our Saviour and heavenly Father respectively.

5. Christian Prayer

Step 1: Recognition and Appeal

This is the mandatory remembrance of our sinfulness, which leads to a plea for forgiveness through faithful recognition and confession. It is also a prayer of thankfulness to the Holy Spirit for being our advocate with the heavenly Father, through the mediation of his Son our Lord and Saviour. This provides an opportunity to recognise the debt owed to the Holy Spirit for deigning to enter our blemished hearts and for condemning our sinful state, before leading us to confession and repentance of all sin. He will cleanse us by washing our bodies with pure water and by pouring the love of God into our sinful hearts (Ro. 5:5). This is his process of sanctification by faith alone (Ro. 4:5, 5:1, 9:30; Gal. 2:16) through humbling the soul and making one appear righteous in God's sight (Ge. 15:6).

It also provides an opportunity to express a personal petition of gratitude to the Holy Spirit for opening our spiritual eyes to recognise the glory of the risen Lord. His light shines down to penetrate the gloom of despondency and despair in one's daily pilgrimage. The Holy Spirit facilitates our spiritual entry into God's celestial Temple, by lifting up our souls to the Gate of Paradise (Jn. 10:9). Through Christ's grace we may enter his courts with praise and be led by our mediator into the sanctuary of his most holy presence, to praise and give thanks to God our Father.

Step 2: Adoration

This is a voluntary offering of thanksgiving for our forgiveness and redemption. We gain forgiveness through recognition of Christ's suffering or passion and our redemption through his sacrificial reconciliation (Isa. 53:10–12). It includes an adoration of God's faithfulness, love and forgiving grace, as revealed to us by Christ. This is the foundation of our profound love and thanksgiving, which we render to our Saviour and Redeemer. The approach requires our spiritual entry into the very presence of the risen Lord; for only this communion provides a personal opportunity to acknowledge his grace. We give thanks for his gift of expiation, or 'the blotting out' of our sins. This is by the divine process of substitutional atonement, for which Christ demands a personal plea for forgiveness. This enables him by imputation to accept our sins, as he is the perfect sinless offering to the heavenly Father.

Our debt for his forgiving grace is repaid by personally visiting his cross on Golgotha, to witness Christ's atoning sacrifice, as a sin or burnt offering to appease the wrath of God. We should be prepared to spiritually suffer and die with him, in order to be buried and raised through him spotless, reconciled and acceptable in the sight of his heavenly Father (Col. 2:11–15)!

This stage involves the completion of our purification, through the death and resurrection of our Saviour, the Lord Jesus Christ. Our confession is rewarded by his redemption from all sin through the shedding of his precious blood. It creates a new pathway through the torn curtain, into the Most Holy Place of the inner sanctuary of the heavenly Tabernacle.

The Lord Jesus Christ is our High Priest who mediates for all believers, as he sits at the right hand of his heavenly Father in the unapproachable seventh heaven. Our Saviour intercedes on our behalf, in the very presence of God in his Holy of Holies; (Heb. 7:25, 8:1–2; 1 Jn. 2:1–2) our names are continuously present upon his lips (Alec Motyer)!

Step 3: Supplication

This is a second voluntary offering of thanksgiving for the fulfilment of the first and second parts of our prayer. It must be presented even before a personal entry into the most holy presence to commune with the heavenly Father, as instructed by Jesus Christ in the Lord's Prayer.

This final act of worship and praise involves a spiritual entry into the Most Holy Place of the heavenly Tabernacle to present our praises and petitions; for it is only there that we can commune with the heavenly Father through the mediation of his Son. Such a privileged approach into the very presence of God our Father (1 Th. 3:9, 13) provides an opportunity to present our peace or fellowship offering. Recognition of God's holiness is by faith alone. Belief in our heavenly Father's justification and salvation is a divine mystery, as this privilege is far beyond all human understanding and endeavours. It is a gift from God that is freely given, being the reward for our personal belief in the atoning power of his Son, Jesus Christ (Ro. 3:25–26).

Every believer should fulfil the mandatory act and also the first voluntary act of worship before daring to attempt to enter the most holy presence of the heavenly Father. This may not be considered to be the only pathway of prayer, but it never fails to gain a warm reception. Such a divine revelation of heavenly reconciliation enables even a sinful and repentant believer to commune with the heavenly Father in and through Christ's name. These principles and steps are embraced in a personal spiritual prayer included in the Appendix.

6. Final Thoughts, before Prayer

Previous to his teaching of the Lord's Prayer, Jesus had taken refuge from the pressing crowd of followers by retreating up a hill overlooking the Sea of Galilee, not far from Capernaum. His disciples followed and he first taught them the principles of Christian faith, highlighting the hallmarks of faith found in every citizen under the rule of his kingly reign (Mt. 5:3–10). Again he listed the essential features of their faith in ascending order, from the lowest to the highest levels in a spiritual and logical sequence.

"Blessed are the poor in spirit, for theirs is the kingdom of heaven.
Blessed are those who mourn, for they will be comforted.
Blessed are the meek, for they will inherit the earth."

Therefore, the first hallmark of all Christian saints is complete humility by being poor in spirit. It is the product of a continual awareness of their inherent sinful nature, which is an offence to the heavenly Father. This humility stimulates a desire to mourn over past sinful deeds, leading to a personal rejection of pride and arrogance, followed by the Scriptural confession and repentance, "God have mercy on me, a sinner" (Lk. 18:13).

Humble yourselves, therefore, under God's mighty hand,
that he might lift you up in due time. Cast all your anxiety on him because he cares for you."
(1 Pe. 5:6–7)

For God opposes the proud, but shows favour to the meek, humble and oppressed (Pr. 3:34).

Following this expression of personal humility, another hallmark of Christian faith is the possession of a deep desire to be free from sin and all its consequences in our lives.

Until we realise' the impurity of our own hearts, we cannot begin to plead for the miraculous cleansing power of our Saviour and Redeemer through his precious blood.

"Blessed are those who hunger and thirst after righteousness, for they shall be filled."

Primarily, this 'metamorphosis' or personality transformation demands a total emptying of all wickedness through the process of justification and sanctification, both being free gifts of the heavenly Father through faith in Jesus Christ. Once free from all personal sin, the vacuum created is over-filled with his divine love. Christian survival is totally dependent upon the enduring love of God, as revealed in Jesus Christ. This follows and even pursues us throughout our lives (Ps. 23:6 *see* N.I.V.fn.)

Such a foundation of faith keeps reminding us of one of the Apostle Paul's confessions,

"No, in all these things we are more than
conquerors through him who loved us.
For I am persuaded, that neither death nor life,
neither angels nor demons,
neither the present nor the future; nor any powers,
neither height nor depth, nor anything in all creation,
will be able to separate us from the love of God
that is in Christ Jesus our Lord."
(Ro. 8:37–39)

Following the mourning over personal sinfulness, the awareness of an impure heart and thirsting for the righteousness, the final and ultimate hallmark of Christian faith is the gradual realisation of an overwhelming desire to see God!

"Blessed are the pure in heart, for they shall see God."

In Scripture the heart is meant to be the centre of our being, involving our personality from which evolves our affections and emotions, our intellect and will. Purity is never gained by human endeavour, but is the outcome of God's miraculous conversion of our sinful hearts (Rev. 21:7). This means being without evil, cleansed or undefiled and single-hearted by having one overriding purpose (Eph. 6:5; Rev. 22:14. K.J.V.). Therefore, to be pure in heart is being like Jesus,

"Who did no sin, neither was guile found in his mouth."
(1 Pe. 2:21–22K.J.V.)

To be pure in heart demands a total obedience to the first commandment, "be holy, because I am holy" (Lev. 11:44).

"Make every effort to be holy, for without holiness no one will see the Lord."
(Heb.12:14)

No man can see God physically, as God is Spirit. But with the eye of faith, Christians can see the hand of God in this world, as in nature and personal experiences during their own lives. By faith Moses persevered, because he recognised the physical evidence of the invisible God (Heb. 11:27).

It has been said that a vision of God is the '*summum bonum*' or the ultimate goal of Christian faith (Ps. 27:4). Philip expressed the deep feelings of the disciples when he said, "Lord, show us the Father and that will be enough for us." But Jesus answered,

"Don't you know me, Philip? Anyone who has seen me has seen the Father."

(Jn. 14:8-9)

Only a chosen few are blessed with a vision of the Son of God in this world, as most believers must wait for our final glorification before we are rewarded with this encounter.

John reminded us,

"But we know that when Christ appears, we shall be like him, for we shall see him as he is. All who have this hope in him purify themselves just as he is pure."

(1 Jn. 3:2–3)

This final hallmark of Christian belief demands a total and constant awareness of the faithfulness of the Triune God towards those he has chosen.

"We know in all things God works for the good of those who love him,
who have been called according to his purpose.
For those who God foreknew, he also predestined to be conformed to the image of his Son, that he might be the first of many brothers and sisters.
And those he predestined, he also called; those he called he also justified
and those he justified he also glorified."

(Ro. 8:28–30)

So let us humble ourselves before the Triune God, in recognition of his faithfulness, love and forgiving grace towards all repentant sinners; to worship and pay homage to him in our prayers at the beginning of each day, as Jesus practised throughout his worldly pilgrimage (Mk. 1:35).

The experience is awesome, but God is gentle and kind. His holiness is perfection in comparison to our poor reflection, but he is gracious and forgiving. His righteousness is unyielding, but he is merciful to those who fear his name and trust him with all their hearts. He is faithful and knows our every need before the words are on our lips (Ps. 139:4) yet he delights to listen to faltering and truthful prayers.

So let us worship him in humble prayer!

APPENDIX

The Nicene Creed

**We believe in one God,
The Father, the Almighty.
Maker of heaven and earth,
Of all that is seen and unseen.**

**We believe in one Lord, Jesus Christ,
The only Son of God,
Eternally begotten of the Father,
God from God, Light from Light,
True God from true God.
Begotten, not made, of one Being with the Father;
Through him all things were made.**

**We believe in the Holy Spirit,
The Lord, the giver of Life,
Who proceeds from the Father and the Son,
Who with the Father and the Son is worshipped and glorified.**

It is generally accepted that this Creed is based on the apostolic declaration of Christian belief, recorded in step with the unfolding of God's plan of redemption revealed throughout their lives spent in the ministry of the Gospel of Jesus Christ.

PRAYERS TO THE HOLY SPIRIT

Prayer of St. Augustine

'Holy Spirit, love of God, who proceedeth from the Almighty Father and His most Blessed Son, powerful Advocate, and sweetest Comforter, infuse Thy grace, and descend plentifully into my heart; for in whomsoever Thou dwellest, the Father and Son come likewise and inhabit that breast which is honoured with so glorious and so Divine a guest, in whose company the Father and Son take up their abode. Oh come, Thou cleanser of all inward pollution, and healer of all spiritual wounds and diseases! Come Thou strengthener of the feeble knees and raiser up of them that fall.

Come, Thou star and guide of them that sail in this tempestuous sea of the world. Thou only Haven of the tossed and shipwrecked. Come Thou glory and crown of the living; Thou only stay and shield of the dying. Come, in much mercy. Come, and make me feel fit to receive Thee. And all this I beg for the sake of Jesus, my only Saviour, who, in unity of Thee, O Holy Spirit, liveth and reigneth with the Father, one God, world without end. Amen'

(Gems of Thought Page 333)

Prayer of Dr. Martyn Lloyd-Jones

'Spirit of God, descend upon my heart;
Wean it from earth; through all its pulses move;
Stoop to my weakness, mighty as Thou art,
And make me love Thee, as I ought to love.

Teach me to love Thee as thine angels love,
One holy passion filling all my frame –
The baptism of the heaven – descended Dove,
My heart an altar. And Thy love the flame.'

(The Christian Warfare. Eph. 6:10, Page 275)

PERSONAL PRAYER

RECOGNITION AND APPEAL TO THE HOLY SPIRIT

'Holy Spirit, Eternal Lord,
gift from the heavenly Father, through Jesus Christ our Saviour.
Purchaser of the eternal life from the world to come, to give to those who proclaim Jesus is Lord of their lives in this world.
May your Holy presence descend upon us this day, to be so very near, in our mouths and in our hearts, that we may hear and obey the Word of our Lord.
Empty us of all our sinfulness and shame, our self-centredness and unfaithfulness,

for we confess and repent of all our sins.
Wash our bodies with pure water, to cleanse us of our daily and nightly stains.
And pour the love of God into our sinful hearts, to purify and sanctify our souls, setting us apart as fit dwelling places for your Holy presence within our hearts today.
Open our spiritual eyes,
to refresh our vision of the radiant glory of the risen Lord, our living God.
May his light so shine down into the depths of our turbulent souls,
to penetrate the gloom of despondency and despair and to enlighten our understanding of his word, his will, his ways and precepts,
that we may learn to love him with all our hearts,
to hunger and thirst after his humility and holiness: to honour, obey and serve him,
for the remainder of our short, uncertain, worldly lives and pilgrimages.
Holy Spirit raise us up to Christ's very presence, the Gate of heaven!
May it be his will that we may enter his courts with praise and through his mediation
to give thanks to our heavenly Father,
for his faithfulness, love and grace that flows to us through Jesus Christ our Saviour,
upon ourselves and those whom we love and cherish in this world, as in the world to come.

ADORATION, IN THE NAME OF JESUS CHRIST

Saviour Lord may it be your will and our supreme privilege, to be led
by the Holy Spirit into your very presence, in the paradisiacal kingdom of heaven.
Clothed in the robes of your humility and righteousness,
to hide our inner sinfulness and prevent us from offending
the glorified ones serving your throne of grace!
As privileged believers from this world, may we be invited
to join the outer fringe of the great holy communion of saints,
including the elders, prophets, apostles and martyrs,
who with the saints of heaven and the angels, bow down and worship,
our Saviour, our Redeemer.
As our Saviour, the Lamb of God, who has taken away the sins of the world,
paying the ransom price through the breaking of his body on the cross of Golgotha.
Victoriously overcoming sin and eternal death for each of us,
by nailing our sins to his cross.
As our Redeemer,
sacrificing his life in this world by the shedding of his precious blood,
to declare righteous those who have suffered and died with him
and have been buried, to be raised through him,

spotless and reconciled in the sight of his heavenly Father.
As blood-bought Christian believers, saved by his grace alone
through his atoning sacrifice, we boldly approach the throne of grace,
to worship and adore our Saviour God, the Lord our Righteousness.
'We are coming to our King.
These large petitions to him we bring.
For his grace and power are such,
None can ever ask too much.'
King of kings and Lord of lords,
we worship you in the beauty of your Holiness,
bowing down before you to proclaim and reflect your glory,
the glory of the One and only begotten Son of the Father,
full of grace and truth.

Sovereign Lord, grant us the supreme honour of being led by your Spirit,
through the veil of your righteousness,
that we may dare enter the Most Holy Place of your heavenly Sanctuary.
For it is only there that we will find the Shekinah, the glory,
of the most holy presence of our heavenly Father.
And it is only there that we may seek his forgiveness,
by offering up our bodies as living sacrifices,
at the mercy seat, ever sprinkled with your blood!
The blood of the Eternal Covenant,

between such an awesome, holy and righteous Father,
and humble sinners, such as we are.
But saved by his grace alone,
and who come in and through the name of Jesus and
in the power of the Holy Spirit.

SUPPLICATION TO THE HEAVENLY FATHER

Abba, Father God, in heaven above,
Holy, holy, holy, Lord!
Pour out your salvation upon your people in this world today
through your Son, Jesus Christ,
that he by his Spirit,
may honour and hallow your most holy Name in our humble hearts;
and we may taste and see that the Lord is good,
to those who fear his most holy name, but trust him with all their hearts!
Awesome, but gentle and kind,
Holy and gracious,
Righteous yet merciful,
to those who love and adore his most holy Name.

Heavenly Father,
may your Holy Spirit descend upon us today,
to bless, anoint and baptise us with the oil of joy and gratitude,
for your enduring love, which flows to us through Jesus Christ?

Holy Father,
may your will be done in our lives in this world, as in heaven above.
Grant us the privilege of being interwoven into the fabric of your eternal plan of salvation,
which unfolds around and before us, as we await the coming of our Lord?
Let not our labours be in vain, but may they find favour in your sight,
and bear fruit for your service in due season.

Gracious Father,
feed us with the heavenly manna and mahar that we may partake and participate,
in the'bread of life and the fruit of the vine', in his Church in this world today,
as he has promised that we will do so at his feast in paradise tomorrow.

Loving Father,
give to us the gift of obedience,
that we may truly forgive those who are indebted towards us,
as you have so often forgiven us of our unfaithfulness and shame.

Righteous Father,
keep us from all evil.
Provide the willpower to contain the evilness within our own hearts,
to prevent it breaking out and separating us from your love;
and the power to rebuke the evil one who lurks around,

luring us into the sinful ways of living we once enjoyed,
before the purity of your love was revealed in Jesus Christ.

Eternal Father,
may we bring to you our personal petitions for today?

We pray,
for your ministers and missionaries at home and abroad in distant lands,
who have dedicated their lives to the spreading of your Gospel,
and for all your people that are persecuted for righteousness' sake.
Strengthen their faith and uphold them in times of need,
as they struggle to spread the boundaries of your kingdom in this world.

We pray,
for our sisters and brothers who are sick;
some who are dying!
We commend them to your loving arms,
knowing that you will never leave them or forsake them.

And we pray,
for those who mourn for the loss of loved ones,
who were with them yesterday, but now are gone.
Comfort them with your eternal promise that they will be resurrected,
on the day that our Lord comes!
For your kingdom, your power and your glory are forever.

The Epilogue

Glorious Father,
we thank you for all the blessings that you have showered upon us,
during our lives in this world,
the honours and privileges, the joys and tears of life,
our health and our strength;
but, most of all,
we are grateful for the indescribable gift of your Son,
our Saviour, Jesus Christ.
And for his Holy Spirit,
whom you have placed within our hearts, to reveal your love in Christ.

Heavenly Father,
we thank you for listening to our prayers,
and hearing the petitions that prove to be acceptable.
Graciously fulfil them in your own way.
And in the world to come,
you have promised,
we will be forever with our Lord and his Holy Spirit in your most Holy presence,
in the paradisiacal Kingdom of Heaven.
"Even so, come, Lord Jesus."
And
May the grace and peace of the Lord Jesus Christ,
the ineffable and unfailing love of our heavenly Father,
and the sweet presence of the Holy Spirit,
be with us all,
today, tomorrow and evermore,
Amen.

REFERENCES

Preface

Aurelius Augustine iii

'The Confessions of Saint Augustine'

Whitaker House

Foreword

Martyn Lloyd-Jones 1

'Sermon on the Mount' Vol. 2.

Inter-Varsity Fellowship

William Hendriksen 3

A Commentary on the Gospel of John. Banner of Truth

OLD TESTAMENT

Chapter 1

John Calvin 11

'Genesis' Banner of Truth

W.M.Thomson, D.D. 17

'The Land of the Book' London. Nelson and Sons.

Origen 19

'Commentary on Matthew'

(quoted in a Dictionary of Biblical Tradition in English Literature)

Chapter 2

Bill Medcalf 47

'The Bible come to Life'

Chapter 3
W.M. Thomson, D.D. 52
'Land of the Book' London. Nelson and Sons.
John Brown 57
'The Epistle to the Hebrews' Banner of Truth.

NEW TESTAMENT

Chapter 4
William Hendriksen 90
Com. on St. John's Gospel
Chapter 5
B.B.Warfield 93
The Person and Work of Christ. 1990
Works of Flavius Josephus
(William Whiston's translation)
J. A. Wilkinson 94
'God's Unfolding Plan of Redemption' Unicorn
Isaac Watts 95
'When I survey the wondrous Cross'
Elizabeth Clephane 98
'Upon the Cross of Jesus'
John Brown 106
'The Epistle to the Hebrews' Banner of Truth
Martin Luther 107
Quoted in New Dictionary of Theology. I.V.P.
Chapter 6
John Pollock 110
'The Apostle'
A Lion Paperback
John Brown 111
'The Epistle to the Hebrews' The Banner of Truth

Chapter 7
Martyn Lloyd-Jones 147
'The Christian Soldier. Vol. 6.
The Harmsworth Encyclopaedia, London. 152
Chapter 8
Spurgeon (1883) 189
A New Biography. The Banner of Truth
Martyn Lloyd-Jones 190
The Christian Soldier. Vol. 6. Banner of Truth.
Martin Luther 197
Quoted in New Dictionary of Theology. I.V.P.
Chapter 9
Alec Motyer 215
'Christ's Prayer for all Believers'
Sermon from Above Bar Church, Southampton.

Appendix
Prayers to the Holy Spirit. 222
St. Augustine 223
Gems of Thought. (p.333)
Martyn Lloyd-Jones 224
Christian Warfare. (p.275)
'Haste my soul, thy suite prepare,
Jesus loves to answer Prayer!' 227
Congregational Church Hymnal.